STRESS-FREE
SAILING

SINGLE AND SHORT-HANDED TECHNIQUES

STRESS-FREE
SAILING

SINGLE AND SHORT-HANDED TECHNIQUES

Duncan Wells

ADLARD COLES NAUTICAL
BLOOMSBURY
LONDON · NEW DELHI · NEW YORK · SYDNEY

To the girls – Sally, Katie and Ellie

Published by Adlard Coles Nautical
an imprint of Bloomsbury Publishing Plc
50 Bedford Square, London WC1B 3DP
www.adlardcoles.com

ADLARD COLES, ADLARD COLES NAUTICAL and the Buoy logo
are trademarks of Bloomsbury Publishing Plc

First published by Adlard Coles Nautical in 2015

ISBN 978-1-4729-0743-1
ePDF 978-1-4729-1975-5
ePub 978-1-4729-1974-8

A CIP catalogue record for this book is available from the British Library.

This book is produced using paper that is made from wood grown in managed,
sustainable forests. It is natural, renewable and recyclable. The logging and
manufacturing processes conform to the environmental regulations of the country
of origin.

Typeset in 10.5 on 13pt Bliss Light
Typesetting and page layout by Susan McIntyre
Printed in China by C&C Offset Printing Co., Ltd.

Note: while all reasonable care has been taken in the publication of this book, the
publisher takes no responsibility for the use of the methods or products described
in the book.

All photographs are by or on behalf of Duncan Wells unless otherwise specified.

CONTENTS

Dawn sun on a starboard mark

ACKNOWLEDGEMENTS

I would like to thank first of all Duncan Kent without whom none of this would have kicked off. Having pitched the monthly yachting magazines in the UK several years ago and not having been bowled over by their response, it was he, as editor of *Sailing Today*, who eventually said: 'OK I'll give you a two-page slot for boat handling articles every month.' It was Duncan again who invited me to the Yachting Journalists' Association's Yachtsman of the Year lunch at Trinity House and introduced me to Janet Murphy of Bloomsbury Publishing.

I then pitched Janet unmercifully to publish my book *Just A Sharp Scratch* about my experience of being shot in the abdomen by a faulty safety flare and surviving what the medics describe as an unsurvivable accident. We nearly got that commissioned and may yet get a publisher. Janet, though, was more interested in my single- and short-handed techniques, which were by then appearing in *Yachting Monthly*, and commissioned me to write this book.

Thanks to John Goode for fixing it for me to speak at the London International Boat Show which allowed me to pitch Bloomsbury for one book, only to be be commissioned for this book.

Thanks too to the lovely Jenny Clark at Bloomsbury who edited with sensitivity and accuracy and produced a much better product than I presented her with. Interestingly she has allowed me to leave that sentence in.

Then thanks to all those who rowed in and helped. I have been absolutely amazed at the fantastic support I have had for this book. Whatever I was doing with *Dorothy Lee*, whatever mad exercise I was conducting, they came over to find out what I was doing, got involved and helped. I am eternally grateful to all of them.

So thank you to:
- Barrie Neilson, of Sailing Holidays, whom I approached for shots of Mediterranean mooring, who just said: 'Well, why not come with us when we go out to Corfu in May and we'll set up the shots you need.' Fantastic.
- Clinton Lyon of Gillingham Marina who gave me the run of the marina to take shots of box mooring. Thanks to Peter and Christine from *Mandurah* and David and Ros from *Demon of Arun* who allowed me to photograph their box mooring techniques.
- Universal Marina who accommodated my every request to try this or that on stretches of pontoon or into and out of berths.
- Justin Hill of Universal Marina.
- Caroline at Chantereyne Marina Cherbourg.
- Alan Barwell for the chats about knots, especially the Prusik knot, which led me to discover the Klemheist.
- John Lewis Partnership Sailing Club for allowing me to hang my boat, at alarming angles, off their boats.
- The boat owners who allowed me to go out sailing with them or adorn their boats in string and try this and that:
  Victor and Pat from *Layla Ann*
  David from *Elinor*
  Sue and Matthew from *Southern Cross*
  Ken and Barbara from *Capricorn*
  And special thanks to Giles and Pauline from *Quintessence* and their sailing school Ocean Adventures Sailing for their tremendous support.
- Alex Whitworth who always keeps me on the straight and narrow.
- The friends who have come with me, held cameras, taken shots, helped with photo shoots, given advice: Robert Chippett, Tony Hutson, Vladimir Chorbadzchiev, Richard Strange, Jan Bek, Jonathan Otter, Steve Barber, Jar Vahey, Andrew Rogers and Keith Bater. And to Andy Hobbs for providing his RIB and accompanying us on occasion with the grandest camera boat in the world, a Princess 23m. Shots from the flying bridge are almost aerial!
- Rick Buettner, wonderful photographer, for being so generous with his time and help.
- Lesley France for her fabulous photoshopping.

And finally thanks to my family for allowing me the time to go sailing to find these things out.

A gaff cutter yawl being single-handed

PREFACE

This book is very different from any other sailing manual you will have come across. Not only do we present ground-breaking single-handed techniques for getting on and off berths (including tiny, wobbly French finger berths), picking up and dropping mooring buoys and box mooring, we also present the answer to man overboard retrieval with MOB Lifesavers from Duncan Wells (www.moblifesavers.com) and provide video links to show some of the described techniques in action. Throughout the book you will see a symbol like this ▯ and the words 'scan this QR code to watch a video on...'. If you have a smart phone or tablet and a quick response (QR) code reader app, which you can download for free, then you scan the QR code and the video will play on your device. If you don't have a phone or tablet you can go to westviewsailing.co.uk/stress-free-videos and view the videos there.

A little about me: I am 60 years old. I still haven't decided what I am going to do when I grow up. I started in advertising and moved into performance as a voice-over actor, something I have done for the past 30 years. We had a dinghy at home that got sailed about twice when I was young. I learned to windsurf. I went with friends on their 20-foot motorboat which we would trail to rivers and the sea, to Salcombe mostly. I vowed to buy a big Princess motor cruiser one day and ended up many years later buying one to introduce the family to boating.

As a teenager I sailed on a few racing boats, spent ages sitting on the weather rail being fed Mars bars every now and then and watching as the skipper and the expert crew managed to broach the boat often enough to bust the spinnaker, which pleased the novice crew enormously as from that point the broaching business stopped.

Prior to taking my family out on the water I did my RYA Day Skipper theory and practical and then Yachtmaster theory. The family weren't all that fussed about the motor boat so I swapped her for a sailing boat, sailed all over the place and did my Yachtmaster MCA exam. Then it was on to be an RYA instructor and setting up my own sail training business, Westview Sailing. I often tell people that I am only an instructor so I don't forget it all, which I would be bound to do if teaching the subject didn't keep me on the money.

In April 2006 I was shot in the abdomen by a faulty collision warning flare while making a film about the correct way to deploy safety and emergency flares. Nine months in hospital followed. The flare also went through my right hand, but that has been stitched back together beautifully. To look at me, apart from the fact that I am extremely overweight, you wouldn't notice a thing. The NHS and one's body can achieve remarkable things.

Today we just stick with the shore-based courses at Westview and we offer video tutorials that cover all of the shore-based navigational disciplines. RYA students find these very useful as study aids – www.westviewsailing. co.uk/videotutorials. These are also available as an app, which allows students to take these videos out on the water with them.

I hope you enjoy the book and find the techniques useful. I use them every time I go sailing. If you have any ideas you'd like to share or improvements to what I suggest please do not hesitate to contact me.

DW

INTRODUCTION & PHILOSOPHY

I take great comfort from reading in Eric Hiscock's *Wandering Under Sail* 'that I bought my boat on a Wednesday, sailed her away on Thursday and found her wrecked on Friday is an unfortunate fact'. Then there was Joshua Slocum on *Spray* who managed to clout someone as he exited the harbour at the start of his three-year circumnavigation. Nobody was ever born a master mariner. Even the greats had to learn the hard way, just like us.

I do not have salt running through my veins, neither do I have a great deal of money, so I have had to be careful with my boating. I haven't done it on a shoe string either; I've just tried to look after what I have. You can glean a great deal of useful information about the best pieces of kit to buy, what you really need and what you don't by reading the books of blue water sailors and liveaboards. Lin and Larry Pardey's books are an invaluable source, as is Annie Hill's *Voyaging on a Small Income*. I often refer to Eric Hiscock's *Cruising under Sail* and Bill and Laurel Cooper's *Sell up and Sail* is a must for anyone dreaming of the great escape. I particularly like the Pardeys' advice to prospective voyagers to 'go small, go simple, go now'.

Never tell anyone that you are going to sail around the world or go on a long trip (unless, of course, you are signed up for a Challenge boat or a Clipper or have entered an OSTAR race), because if you put your nose out around the headland, decide it is not for you and head for home, you do look a bit of a Charlie. I can number half a dozen boats as one sails down the Hamble that have gone no further. Round-the-world sailors, Mediterranean cruisers who are still here, departing one day. So if you plan to sail around the world, tell people you are going to make a trip to Lisbon and see how it goes from there. It's worth telling them you are going a reasonable distance because to announce that you are

going for a spin round the bay will have them calling the emergency services if you haven't returned by tea time. Still, we are getting ahead of ourselves.

Now I am sure that I am not going to tell the seasoned sailors among you anything you do not already know. I may remind you of things that you had forgotten and I may raise issues for consideration. For those new to sailing I am hoping that what I offer will go a long way to making your time on the water that much more enjoyable. I am assuming that we all know how to sail and so will be sharing those tips, techniques and systems I have discovered that help to make sailing stress-free. I don't have all the answers and there is rarely only one way of doing things, but what I illustrate has been tested by me and works for me.

I used to tell my students that boating is just a matter of lurching from one crisis to the next. What we have to do is to take the drama out of it. I have now adapted this statement to say that it *can* be a matter of lurching from one crisis to the next because if we concentrate on becoming confident in our boat handling and sailing and seamanlike in our approach, we will reduce the chance of having a crisis. And so we start.

WHY LEARN SINGLE-HANDED TECHNIQUES?

I tell folk who set out to be sailors that if they want to take up sailing for life they had better learn the single-handed techniques because sure as eggs is eggs they will be single-handing one day. This could be early on after they have frightened the entire family away or later on as the last remaining family member begins to make excuses.

Case in point

This man has invited his family to join him on a charter boat for the weekend. He has just completed an RYA Day Skipper course, a nine-day intensive shore-based and practical combined, and he stands before us declaring that we can trust our lives to him out on the water.

This confidence has been inspired by the fact that on the five-day practical part of the course there were four other able-bodied students who knew a little about what was going on and an instructor to tell them what to do. Now the new skipper has three hands – a wife and two children – that haven't a clue what is happening and no instructor to tell him what to do.

What will happen now is that he will scare them half to death and he may well lose them as crew for ever. Many is the time I see berth holders in my marina arrive on their own. 'No Marjorie today?' I call. 'Ah, well you see we had a bit of an incident last time and she has been rather put off by it', is the standard reply.

I should add that an RYA course is extremely valuable and is where everyone should start. That's how I started: Day Skipper theory, then the practical and so on to Yachtmaster.

So what can we do to help ourselves become confident at handling our boat? Remember the upside to all this is that if we are competent and confident this will encourage our crew and we may well be able to keep them sailing with us for longer or at least until other diversions attract their attention. Having daughters, it was a defining day when I spotted an unfeasibly large pair of trainers by the front door. Boating would have to work hard to win out against that sort of competition. Of course, it is possible that after a while the unfeasibly large pair of trainers might be invited to join us for a sail, but that has never been a great success. The daughter in question will spend the whole time texting her friends about how absolutely 'gorge' the unfeasibly large pair of trainers is, while he sits there lumplike, basking in the adoration, neither of them much use as crew.

We will look at single-handed techniques because if we can master these, we are in business. Single-handing is about being self-sufficient, being able to handle the boat in any situation without having to rely on anyone else. And if we can do that on our own, think how much easier and fun it will be to do it with another person or other people. And, of course, single-handing isn't just for single-handers. We can also find ourselves managing things on our own if a partner is looking after children down below or preparing a meal, if our crew have succumbed to the debilitating *mal de mer* or if we have had a tough time of things and the crew are tired.

What's the one thing that gets everyone going? Correct, mooring; getting off and then back on to the dock. We will look at single-handed techniques for these first. We have to perform these manoeuvres in public, of course. You might not think so to look at the marina – there is not a soul about as you prepare to depart. But make a cock-up and heads will pop up all around. People will emerge from companionways fender in hand, desperate to protect their precious boats from the marauding danger that is you.

Lesson one: no shouting, no raised voices, no over-revving of the engine, no furious bow thrusting, no exclamation of 'darling!' with a slight edge to it. And if you do make a bit of a mess of things and end up resting on your neighbour, tie a short line between the two of you amidships to stop the tide pushing you into or out of the berth. Pretend that this is nothing, perfectly acceptable, that you are in control. It's a little difficult to get away with this if the neighbour happens to be having an afternoon gin aboard at the time and in bumping his boat you manage to spill it, but sang froid might get you out of any number of scrapes.

If I ever get it 'not quite right' I step off, line in one hand, camera in the other, and start taking shots. Apart from the fact that these might always be useful for future articles, it gives the impression to any onlooker that my boat hanging somewhat alarmingly off my neighbour's might just have been intentional. I am unlikely to let on. Oh, I just have. If you have a fairly professional-looking camera so much the better. If you have crew you could ask them to pose. Then I warp the boat back to her berth. Always get the line under a cleat to get some decent purchase when hauling in anything heavy like a boat, especially if you want to make it look effortless.

Referring to the techniques as single- and short-handed is slightly confusing. Single-handed means one person. Short-handed means having at least one other hand with hopefully two hands, as it were. And that extra pair of hands makes an enormous difference. We will be looking at exercises and situations from a single-handed point of view initially. Once mastered single-handed, these will then become a good deal easier, indeed a breeze, with two people.

As single- or short-handers we have to plan carefully, we have to prepare properly and we have to be able to anticipate. Planning is just deciding what we want to do. Preparation is the key to it all. Prepare every little thing in advance so it all goes smoothly. Every time something goes wrong for me it is because I didn't prepare properly. Anticipation comes partly from our preparation (we prepared and so we know what will happen) and partly from experience.

TEST BOATS

I have taken several very different boats and tested the techniques on all of them in most wind and tide conditions. Even though you may very well have a different type of boat and experience different conditions, I think you will find that the techniques will work for you. And if they are not exactly right straight out of the box, then I suggest that you experiment to refine them. At the very least I hope that by presenting the various techniques you will be inclined to think about what might work for you.

At the modern end, we tested the techniques on a new Dufour 375 (*Layla Ann*). She is very light and has very high topsides, so it is a long way down to the dock. In fact, it is so far that I found it quite difficult getting aboard – a fender step can help here. The adage 'if you can't step off, don't get off' was never more apt than for this boat. We do not leap ashore from any boat in my book and we certainly do not want to do this from *Layla Ann*. At the traditional end, we tried the techniques on a couple of long keelers.

Here are the boats who came out to play:

- *Layla Ann*, a Dufour 375: bulb keel, sail drive, spade rudder, freeboard 120cm
- *Dorothy Lee*, a Hallberg Rassy 352: long fin keel, shaft drive, skeg-hung rudder, freeboard 110cm, a heavy boat
- *Quintessence*, a Bavaria 42: medium fin winged keel, shaft drive, spade rudder, freeboard 120cm
- *Capricorn*, a Beneteau 321: medium draught, bulbed fin keel, shaft drive, spade rudder, freeboard 110cm
- *Elinor*, a Contessa 26: long keeler, freeboard 60cm
- *Southern Cross*, a Rustler 36: long keeler, freeboard 80cm

Four of the test boats: (clockwise from top left) Southern Cross, Elinor, Layla Ann, Quintessence

SKILLS & DISCIPLINES

To single-hand or short-hand a boat we need to be armed with a tool kit of knowledge and skills that will make our life easier. Single-handing or short-handing relies on using the most effective and quickest way of doing things, that is handy short cuts. So let's look at the few straightforward skills that we'll need. We start with rope because this is at the heart of all boating.

ROPE

We use a lot of this on a sailing boat. We use it to control the sails. We use it when mooring. So what type of ropes do we have, what do we use them for and what is the difference between them?

Care of ropes

Generally you should stow ropes out of sunlight because of UV degradation, but that said my polyester braid jib sheets hang on my pulpit all year round and have done for the past ten years and they appear to be in good shape. They do have a low degradation rating according to the chart. Polypropylene rope left in the sun will simply go white and flake away. Of course, running rigging is exposed to UV the whole time and there is nothing one can do about that, except to check it regularly for chafe and wear.

Mooring lines

Tradition had it that mooring lines benefited from a bit of stretch and so nylon was used, but actually you don't need a lot of stretch for mooring and polyester is much harder-wearing than nylon. This is why warps with pre-spliced eyes are usually made from polyester rope. Now they manufacture rope for warps using a polyester core and a loose polyester braid outer to add in a bit of stretch.

1 Polyester braid specially made for mooring warps: high stretch and hard wearing

2 Polyester, three-strand: used for mooring warps

3 Polyester, braided: used for sheets and halyards

4 Polyester, double-braided: used for sheets and halyards

5 Nylon multiplait: used for anchor warps

6 Polypropylene: used for sports and safety equipment

7 Polypropylene used to re-rig HMS Victory as it looks like hemp

8 Dyneema core: used for sheets and halyards

9 Dyneema core in a polyester braided outer: used for sheets and halyards

ROPES AT A GLANCE

Name	Stretch	Use	UV rating	Sinks/floats
Polyester braid mooring	High	Mooring warps	5	Sinks
Polyester three-strand	Low	Mooring warps	5	Sinks
Polyester braid standard	Low	Sheets and halyards	5	Sinks
Nylon three-strand	High	Anchor cable and mooring warps	4	Sinks slowly
Nylon multi-plait	Very high	Anchor cable and mooring warps	4	Sinks slowly
Polypropylene	Low	Safety and sports gear	2	Floats
Kevlar	Very low	Sheets and halyards	3	Sinks
Dyneema/Spectra	Very low	Sheets and halyards	5	Floats (sinks when in a polyester braid outer)
Vectran	Very low	Sheets and halyards	3	Sinks

UV rating: 5 degrades slowly, 1 degrades quickly

Modern polyester braid: feels good but snags easily. Still, it looks nice

⌘ **Hang them up.** Ropes get wet and they dry quicker if we hang them up.

⌘ Here someone has made a **rack** from which they can hang rope in their cockpit locker. This is a great idea because drips from the rope will drain into the bilges. It's also much tidier than piling ropes one on top of another in the locker.

⌘ **Keep them clean**. Fortunately in northern Europe we get plenty of rain so the standing rigging generally has the salt washed out of it on a regular basis. Once a year I put my polyester braid jib sheets into the washing machine. According to the experts this is OK, as long as you use a gentle wash. I put the jib sheets in a pillow case, but the top needs to be tied; otherwise they escape and start thrashing round inside the washing machine. Use the most fragrant soap powder and the softest softener possible to make the ropes nice to handle.

One of the first things we learn about rope is that it will catch on every potential obstacle in its path. It will twist and kink if we don't coil or lay it out carefully. For a single-hander it requires more attention, and causes more delay, than anything else. You're standing at the bow un-reeving the jib sheet to coil it and hang it on the pulpit when it snags as it runs through a block on the genoa track and you have to go aft and sort it out. Even with the best preparation, rope has a propensity to snag. So we need to do everything in our power to allow lines to run free and preparation of rope is the key to this.

Free running lines

When you want a line to run free you can flake it on to the deck. Make sure there are no knots or creases in it and make what I call an 'intelligent pile', that's where we put down first that which we require last, and it will run free every time. Make intelligent piles for reefing lines, halyards and main sheets – any line that we want to run out snag-free.

We can also prepare figure of eight coils by hand laying the rope out. We put that which we require last down first and then coil the rope in a figure of eight on

Intelligent piles

top. You can also do this with the aid of a winch or a windlass – see box opposite.

Larger boats with longer lines will always coil them the figure of eight way because this is the more foolproof way of doing things. There is always the chance that a large pile of flaked line could fall over and ruin the free-running effect. This cannot happen with figure of eight coils. This is the more seamanlike way of preparing a rope to run free.

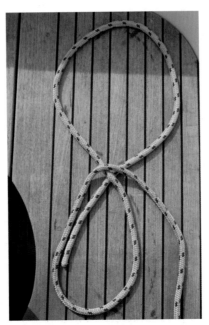

Starting off a figure of eight coil

The finished figure of eight coil

FIGURE OF EIGHT COIL WITH THE AID OF A WINCH OR A WINDLASS

  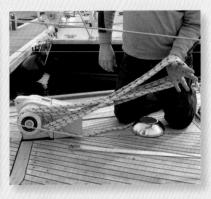

■ With the end of the rope, the bit you will want last on the deck, take the rope over and around the windlass in an anti-clockwise direction and up to our left hand.

■ Go round this in a clockwise direction back down to the windlass and go round this anti-clockwise and build up our figure of eight.

■ A beautiful figure of eight, which will run out freely.

Snag-free coils

There are two ways to coil a rope – the sailor's way and the climber's way. Of the two, the climber's way is the coil least likely to end up in a tangle if dumped on the deck.

The sailor's way

Start with any eye splice or snap shackle first. For neatness this is kept on the inside of the coil. We will make the coils at least as long as in the pictures to the right. All rope needs to be coiled clockwise, whether it be braid or three-strand. If you coil against the twist of the stranding then you're in danger of opening out the rope. When the rope is coiled correctly it feels right, natural and relaxed and it will hang in nice loops.

Start with the eye splice on the inside of the coil

Coil the rope clockwise, keeping even loops

To help three-strand lie nicely you need to give a little twist, a half turn of the hand, as you make each loop. With stranded rope you can feel that it wants to do this, so go with the direction of the twist. Then, leaving some rope still available, make a few turns or wraps round the coils. Now it is a question of how we finish off. We have the gasket coil hitch and then what I call the sailor's way and the Navy way (see photos below).

If we are coiling braided rope we will find that it often forms itself naturally into a figure of eight. Don't fight this, just let it happen if that's what the rope wants to do.

Braided rope often naturally forms a figure of eight

Navy way, gasket coil hitch, sailor's way – note how the gasket coil hitch does not hang very nicely

⌘ **Gasket coil hitch:** Take a bight through the coils. Take this over the top of the coils and pull down tight. The gasket coil hitch won't come undone in the locker, but it is a bit inelegant when hung up. So, if I am going to hang up my ropes I will use the sailor's or the Navy way.

A finished gasket coil hitch

Finishing a coil the sailor's way

⌘ **Sailor's way:** Take a bight through the coils as before, but instead of folding this down over the coil take the running end through this.

Finishing a coil the Navy way

⌘ **Navy way:** Having made a few wraps around the coils simply take the running end through between the wraps and the top of the coils.

Coiling the climber's way

Jib sheets coiled the climber's way

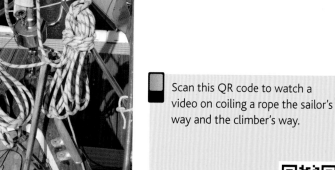

Scan this QR code to watch a video on coiling a rope the sailor's way and the climber's way.

The climber's way

The first coil goes into the hand and the second coil goes between the thumb and forefinger. As you keep doing this you are getting loops of line on either side.

I keep my jib sheets on the pulpit in this manner. That way they are off the deck, cannot accumulate dirt and I can hose them down to get rid of the salt with ease. A simple clove hitch on the pulpit does the trick. Of course, I keep them inside the rail – we wouldn't want anything to slip into the drink by accident.

HANGING A ROPE ON A MAST CLEAT

■ Prepare the coils as for coiling a rope the normal sailor's way and then allow a good foot of spare rope at the standing end.

■ Bring a bight of this standing part through the coils.

■ Twist it once.

■ Hook it over the cleat. The halyard will be neatly stowed.

Cheesed spare line

Spare line wrapped over the guard rail

Hung-up spare line

Tidying up spare line

If we have a good deal of line/mooring warp left over we can tidy this in a number of ways. We can cheese it, wrap it over the guard rail or hang it up.

Cheesing is very pretty, but any line lying on the deck for any length of time will get wet and collect dirt. I always think cheesing belongs to the superyacht brigade with crew who spend their time permanently washing and polishing things. Wrapping the line over the rail works fine as does hanging it up, although a wrap never undoes nicely. Where a coil can be flaked out neatly, I always find that a wrap requires me to start from scratch.

ATTACHING TO THE DOCK

Where a line has a pre-spliced eye, we keep this on board, always. It is always the free end that goes on to the dock. This is a key part of being prepared. All lines must be free to run; a line with a pre-spliced eye in it or a loop will catch on something as we bring it back on board – guaranteed. So eyes stay on board.

Even the free end of a line can wrap itself around a shore side cleat alarmingly quickly if we haul it in too quickly or, worse, try to flip it off a cleat. Flipping never works when you want it to. So rather than try to flip a line off just haul in steadily. If you are ever running bridles or slipped lines and a certain amount of line will be passing across the deck, make sure to keep the decks as clear as possible, with as few opportunities for the line to snag as possible.

So you attach the pre-spliced eye to the on-board cleat. This is the standing end of the line. If you don't have eyes in the ends of your mooring lines or warps, you can make a loop by tying a bowline. Or you can OXO the line on to the on-board cleat (see box opposite).

Eyes always stay on board

The eye of the warp goes over the on-board cleat

Here a bowline loop has been used to make fast to the on-board cleat

OXO

This method really does work. It saves a lot of fuss and looks neat.

■ Lead the line around the cleat.

■ Make a complete turn around the cleat: O.

■ Cross over to make the first half of the X.

■ And again to complete the X.

■ Finish with another complete turn around the cleat for the second O. Some braids may need a hitch as well.

 Scan this QR code to watch a video on OXOing a line around a cleat.

An OXO will not undo, it will not tighten on itself over time and it can be undone under load. Of course, you want to feel comfortable that you've left your pride and joy safe, so adding in a hitch is perfectly acceptable, but you don't need it – the OXO will be perfectly secure without it with most types of rope. The only exceptions might be some braids or braid outers such as those that cover Dyneema, which can slip and usually benefit from a hitch on the end of the OXO. However, you're unlikely to be using very expensive Dyneema for mooring warps. If you're going to add a hitch, tie it so it lies down with the lay of the rope on the top of the OXO. This is the seamanlike way.

I am told that an OXO can tighten itself from the bottom up if you have a very big boat straining at her warps as she is moved by the tide. And you may find that a hitch has seized. I have never experienced this, not having owned a big enough boat, but this is why large boats never ever use hitches to finish off their OXOs. Crew on big ships will just take another O around the cleat. Quite often, instead of the second O, a hitch is added with the second part of the X. This looks very neat and I have never known it to fail.

Adding an extra hitch to the OXO

A hitch has been added to the second part of the X in this variant of the OXO

MOORING LINES

We need a bow line, stern line and two springs – a head spring (forward spring, bow spring) to stop the bow moving forward and a back spring (aft spring, stern spring) to stop the stern moving backwards. Purists will say 'one line, one job' and if you have a very large boat that makes a great deal of sense. They will also say that 'each line should be able to be undone from either end under tension'. I'm not sure I am too fussed about that; again, this may apply to large boats. I have never found it necessary on my 35-foot boat.

There are two ways of setting this up. Method 1 is where we use four lines and run a bow line, stern line and then springs from the boat to the dock. This is technically the correct way of doing things. And if one doesn't have a midship cleat this makes sense.

However, if you do have a midship cleat then Method 2 is an option and this can be done using just two warps – from the bow to the dock and up

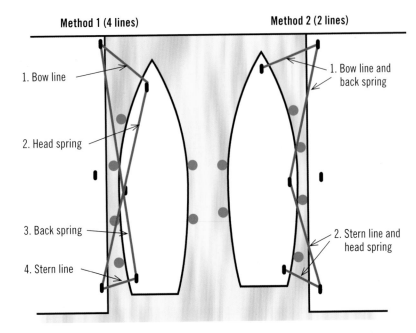

Method 1 (4 lines)

1. Bow line
2. Head spring
3. Back spring
4. Stern line

Method 2 (2 lines)

1. Bow line and back spring
2. Stern line and head spring

Two methods of setting up mooring lines

to the midship cleat for the back spring and from the stern to the dock and up to the midship cleat for the head spring, all tied off with an OXO. Now we are attached securely to the dock – and not a bird's nest in sight. But how are we going to detach ourselves?

◄ *Method 2: mooring with two warps*

▼ *I wonder how long it takes the crew to get this off?*

Slipped lines

We will use slipped lines a great deal. Three points to be aware of with slipped lines:

- Ensure that the amount of line you're hauling in is as short as possible.
- Ensure there is nothing for the line to snag on when you haul it in.
- Lead the line carefully so that the two parts of the line will not rub on each other as you haul in on the inboard end.

 Scan this QR code to watch a video on setting up slipped lines.

Singled up, doubled up *i*

You will hear people refer to slip lines as singled up or doubled up. This is not correct. These are big ship expressions. Doubled up is when they add in a second bow line, stern line, set of breast lines and springs to hold the ship. Singled up is when they get rid of the extra lines and lie to just one bow and stern line and one set of breast lines and springs. In fact, the call from the captain, prior to departure, is often to 'single up to springs', meaning that they will lie to just the one set of spring lines. So if you want the crew to run the lines to the shore and back to the boat ready to be released from on board the instruction should be: 'Make the lines ready to slip, please.' 'Please' always goes down well with crew!

Mooring to tidal quays

We will set lines that are four times the range of the tide in length to allow us to rise and fall with the tide. Generally I set slipped lines so that I can control things from the boat. If I have not allowed enough line then, as the boat falls, I can ease out a bit more. If I tie my lines to the dock I may fall with the tide to a point where it is no longer possible to reach up or climb up to the dock to release the line in the event that I want to leave.

Hauling in a boat on the end of a line

It really is extremely important to get any line under a cleat to get any purchase on it. We have all seen crew crouched in the waterski position trying to haul in 7 tonnes of boat against 20 knots of wind and a wicked tide. The key is to get the line under a cleat. Or if there is significant strain, under one wing of the cleat and over the other. Then, to bring the boat in, haul on the line using your body weight and take up the slack. Do this bit by bit until she is alongside.

Always get the line under a cleat when hauling in a boat

Take up the slack bit by bit until the boat is alongside

Lasso

Preparation is the key to making a lasso work every time. Wetting the line first will often help, to give it some weight. Attach one end of the line to the boat (the standing end), coil the line carefully, divide it in half and hold one half of the coils in one hand, with the other half in the other hand. Make sure the two halves are joined by just one part of the line. Keep ahold of the running end of the lasso in one hand. This should still allow you to throw the coils from that hand. If the line is long enough tie this off to a cleat on board so that both ends are cleated off. We just need enough slack to be able to swing the coils to and fro prior to the throw.

Now when we throw we throw wide. This is important for lassoing success. Then when the rope has landed on the dock, resist the temptation to pull it in quickly as this can make it miss or jump over the cleat you are trying to secure. Haul it in gently, making sure it catches on the wings of the cleat. If you're lassoing from above you need to make sure not to lift the line off the wings of the cleat.

I have seen really practised lasso-ers lasso a cleat at 20 paces from on board. You'll need to have plenty of line, of course. Err on the generous side length-wise. And when it comes to lassoing buoys, try not to lasso them from above as the line can slip off the top of the buoy very easily. If there is a lateral element to the exercise the chance of success is greater, so stand off the buoy a little; this will give the line a chance to bite.

One of the tricky things about lassoing from a boat is that one has to lean over the guard rail or guard wire and we don't get much of a swing going. The answer is wrist action – it's all in the flick of the wrists. Practise this while tied to the dock. Let's see how far you can lasso a pontoon cleat. It will hold you in good stead when you need this skill out on the water.

Throwing a line

In my experience a line thrown to someone often does not get there first time. It always gets there second time. Why? Because when it missed first time it went into the drink and for the second throw the line is wet. It weighs more and it goes further. One way to make it get there first time every time is to throw the line beyond your target. Then it is guaranteed to make the distance.

⌘ To prepare a lasso, attach the standing end of the line to the boat, coil the line carefully, divide it in half and hold one half in each hand.

⌘ Keep ahold of the running end of the lasso in one hand. This should still allow you to throw the coils from that hand.

Here's a rogues' gallery of some of the knots we need. This lot are hitches and bends: cow hitch, clove hitch, slipped clove hitch, round turn and two half hitches, rolling hitch and rustler's hitch

KNOTS

We will need a few knots. Wonderful videos and graphics on how to tie all knots can be found on the internet. I describe here only those for which I have a fondness or a handy way to remember them.

⌘ **Basic seaman's knots:**
Bowline
Clove hitch
Rolling hitch
Sheet bend and double sheet bend
Double fisherman's knot
Round turn and two half hitches
Cow hitch
Slip knot
Figure of eight stopper knot
Stevedore stopper knot

⌘ **Some handy knots from the climbers:**
Figure of eight securing knot
Prusik knot
Klemheist knot

⌘ **The best knot in the whole world and my favourite:**
Rustler's hitch

⌘ **And a party trick to impress the neighbours:**
Tugboat bowline

Bowline

The knot we will probably use most during our boating life. The bowline forms a secure loop at the end of a line. It will not jam. It's easy to undo even after it has been under considerable tension; you just break the back of the knot. If not under tension it can shake loose. Use it for just about everything from tying sheets to a clew, to tying a line to a bucket. Purists will say that it should not be used for mooring because it cannot be undone under tension. This is true, but as long as one end of the mooring warp can be undone under tension I can't see that having a bowline on the other end really matters.

Clove hitch

We use this for tying on fenders. I tie my fenders on with a slipped clove hitch. This comes undone with one tug on the slipped end – invaluable for single- and short-handed sailors. When I set off single-handed I will want to get my fenders in as soon as possible; it is the seamanlike thing to do and so there will be moments in narrow channels when I hand over the helming to George, my trusty autopilot, and I go out on deck to retrieve the fenders. I don't want to be there for longer than necessary, hence the slipped clove hitch. A standard clove hitch would take me far too long to undo.

TYING A BOWLINE

If you can remember a story about a rabbit, a hole and a tree you are in business. The key to the knot is making the 'hole'.

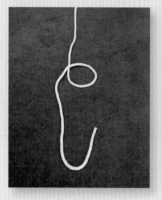 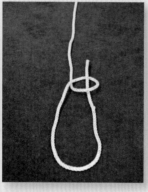 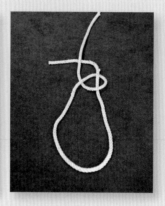 

■ Draw a 6 in the end of the line.

■ Now take the working end of the rope, the 'rabbit', up through the hole.

■ And around the standing part of the rope, the 'tree'.

■ Then back down the hole and pull tight on the three ends and you have a bowline.

CLOVE HITCH OVER A POST OR BOLLARD

■ We make two loops. Twist the rope anti-clockwise for the first loop.

■ And anti-clockwise for the second loop.

■ Now take the second loop over the first loop.

■ And drop over the post or, in this case, winch – and tighten.

Rolling hitch

A knot that binds. The main thing I use this for is tying a snubber to the anchor chain once I have anchored. Traditionally rolling hitches are used for freeing riding turns. Have I ever had to do this? No, but I imagine people have.

Rolling hitches need to be under tension the whole time. If not they can work loose. Ensure that your anchor snubber is tight to keep the rolling hitch locked onto the chain

Sheet bend and double sheet bend

Used for attaching two different thicknesses of line to one another and also just another way of joining two ropes together. I always use a double sheet bend as this won't undo when not under tension, whereas the sheet bend will.

Single sheet bend

Double sheet bend

Double fisherman's

A great knot for joining two pieces of rope together, especially if you're making a line into an endless loop.

Round turn and two half hitches

A knot you can use for mooring. It will undo under tension. It is also useful for tying fenders to stanchions. If we tie them to the base of the stanchion we find that the weight of the fender hanging down tightens the running end of the knot and holds it secure. This is handy in marinas where there is a good deal of movement.

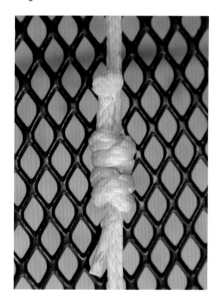

Double fisherman's

A round turn and two half hitches used to tie a fender to the base of a stanchion

Cow hitch

A very pretty knot, but that's about it. It can slip. I use it for hanging wet ropes in the saloon when I want things to be pretty. I have also seen it used successfully (ie it did not slip) for attaching jib sheets and very neat it looks, too.

Cow hitch

Cow hitch used to attach jib sheets to the sail

Slip knot

There are two methods for tying this. Method 1 is traditional. Method 2 is halfway to becoming a bowline and when practised can be quite a party trick. These appear in the video on basic seaman's knots – see QR code right.

Figure of eight stopper knot

For jib sheets and the main sheet only. We don't put stopper knots on spinnaker or cruising chute sheets as these are powerful sails and there may be an occasion when we would need to lose the sail altogether and would want the sheets to run out of the blocks.

Stevedore stopper knot

Another useful stopper knot for sheets, essentially a figure of eight knot that begins with a round turn around the standing part.

Figure of eight securing knot

Climbers use this a lot. It is effectively a double figure of eight knot. We would use this when we were taking someone up the mast in the bosun's chair. Rather than just clip the snap shackle from the spinnaker halyard to a metal ring on the chair we would tie a halyard on with a double figure of eight knot and then snap the shackle to another part of the bosun's chair as a fail safe. Before sending anyone up the mast do have a rig check and ensure that the spinnaker halyard blocks at the top of the mastblock are sound.

Prusik knot

This is another knot that binds. Try it on a steel shroud. Take a couple of

Slip knot

Scan this QR code to watch a video on how to tie the following basic seaman's knots: bowline, clove hitch on a rail, clove hitch over a post, rolling hitch, sheet bend, double sheet bend, double fisherman's, round turn and two half hitches, cow hitch, slip knot method 1, slip knot method 2 into bowline, figure of eight stopper knot and stevedore stopper knot.

▲ *Stevedore to the left, figure of eight to the right.* ▼ *Prusik knot*

metres of line. Tie the ends together so the line is continuous and then take one loop of the line behind the shroud and feed the other end through and repeat four times. When you pull down, the knot does not slip. You can use this for attaching a block to the shroud for the man overboard retrieval system and it is fairly quick to tie.

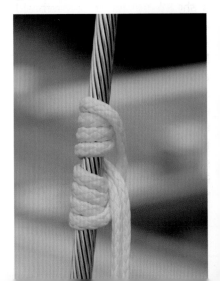

BOSUN'S CHAIR SECURED BY A FIGURE OF EIGHT

   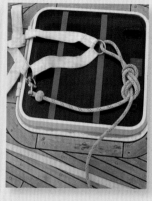

■ Tie a figure of eight knot with plenty of spare.

■ Take the halyard through the ring on the bosun's chair and back to the figure of eight knot.

■ Start following the figure of eight knot and double it up.

■ The finished product with snap shackle tied to a spare ring on the bosun's chair for safety.

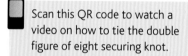 Scan this QR code to watch a video on how to tie the double figure of eight securing knot.

Scan this QR code to watch a video on how to tie the Prusik and Klemheist knots.

Klemheist knot

This is the business when it comes to binding knots. Again, you can use this knot to attach a block to a shroud for the man overboard retrieval system. It takes seconds – about 25 seconds – to tie and locks solid when tension is applied and yet when loosened off can be moved up and down the shroud with ease. Again, use a continuous loop of rope. With the bight at the top, wind the rope around the shroud five times. Take this end and feed it through the bight at the top. Tighten and pull down.

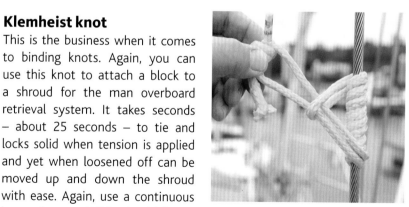

⌘ With the bight at the top, wind the rope around the shroud five times. Take this end and feed it through the bight at the top.

⌘ Tighten and pull down and you have a Klemheist knot.

Slide PVC tubing over stainless steel to give the knot a flat surface to grip on to

A note about Prusik and Klemheist knots. They will bind to anything that is either smooth or rough. When tied to stainless steel rigging which has a twist in it, they can slip if the load is applied gradually. They lock if the load is applied instantly. To prevent slipping, I provide a smooth surface for the knot to grip onto and so I slide a length of PVC tubing over the stainless steel shroud. You can have this pre-rigged.

Rustler's or highwayman's hitch

When you need a line or something on the end of a line, like a fender, in a hurry and yet you want it to be secure until you need it, this is the knot to use. The beauty is that, unlike other knots, the line in the rustler's hitch never actually goes around what you are attaching it to and that is why it will undo instantly. It doesn't look much, but it is a winner. I use it all the time.

I tell people that if we are going to rob a bank and our chosen mode of transport for the day is to be the horse that we will want the horse to be tied up securely to a rail outside the bank while we are about our business and yet when we have extracted the cash we will come flying out of the bank and want the horse to be free with one flick of our wrist. We cannot afford the time to undo a clove hitch or a round turn and two half hitches, we need the rustler's hitch. Is it a strong knot? Well, every time I cross the Channel, Big Bertha, the fender that goes between me and the impending accident, rolls off the

TYING A RUSTLER'S HITCH

■ Take a bight of the line under the rail.

■ Reach through this bight and pick up the standing part.

■ Pull this through and tighten on the running end.

■ Now fingers through the bight you just made.

■ Pick up the running end, pull this through and tighten on the standing end.

■ Now the 'horse' will not get away and yet when you need the line all you have to do is yank on the running end and voilà!

coach roof and hangs over the side and she has never fallen into the drink yet. Better still, I have often used rustler's hitches to hold the boat on to the dock while I drive against them. Purists would have fifty fits, I expect. I don't advocate this, but I have done it in extremis.

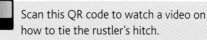
Scan this QR code to watch a video on how to tie the rustler's hitch.

Tugboat bowline

This is a knot that you flick into place and it will give you a loop in the end of a line. I was shown this knot by Justin Hill at Universal Marina and very handy it is, too. When everyone around has shown off their one-handed bowlines, you can really impress them with the tugboat bowline.

Scan this QR code to watch a video on the tugboat bowline.

TUGBOAT BOWLINE PARTY TRICK

■ The start.

■ Flick the running end in the right hand over the two parts of the standing end in the left.

■ Take the bight in your right hand...

■ ... through the bight in your left hand.

■ Pull on the standing end...

... to make the tugboat bowline.

Reef knot/thief knot

There is not much call for the reef knot on a boat. The only thing I use it for is lashing the anchor to the cheeks of the bow roller. But did you know there was a knot that is very like the reef knot? It is just slightly different and it is called the thief knot. The idea was that you would tie up your kit bag with a thief knot and if anyone had undone this and tampered with your belongings, they would be bound to re-tie the kit bag with a reef knot believing that was how it was tied in the first place. And so the owner would know they had been visited by a thief. I did this on a recent flight to Corfu when I tied the handles of my travel grip together like this. And my thief knot was intact at the end. I don't suppose you need to open a bag if you can X-ray it.

Reef knot: both ends on the same side

Thief knot: ends on different sides

BOATHOOK

It seems rather obvious to introduce the boathook, but there are a few things worth mentioning. First, boathooks should only be used for 'hoiking' things out of the briny. They should not be used for collision avoidance or fending off. A decent wooden-shafted boathook with a metal head will punch a hole straight through the GRP of the average modern boat if it is used as a lance. Fortunately, modern boathooks have plastic heads and bendable aluminium shafts so they should self-destruct before they can penetrate the GRP. Always place a fender between you and the impending accident, rather than try to fend off with a boathook. The second thing is that when we want to grab a line, a float or whatever, we need to hold the boathook with the hook towards us, reach beyond what we want to grab, draw it towards us and up for success every time.

HOOKED WITH SUCCESS

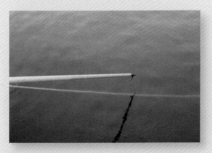

■ Hold the boathook with the hook towards you.

■ Reach beyond what you want to grab.

■ Draw it towards you and up.

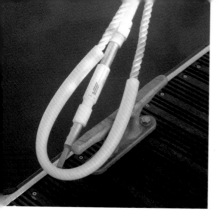

⌘ You can also offer up a bight/loop of line protected in a piece of plastic piping by using the boathook.

⌘ To prevent a line from falling out of the crook, tape its end to the boathook with some insulating tape.

⌘ This insulating tape trick also works with line protected by plastic piping. The beauty is that it won't fall off.

If we have the hook the other way and we come from underneath and outwards we will not always grab the desired object first time and if we do and it does not give we can easily bend the boathook.

We can also use the boathook for offering up a line to a cleat. A boathook is just an extension of our arms. Don't try to over reach with this as it is jolly hard to hold the boathook at arm's length and hope to have any control over it. If you want to get a line on to a cleat at a range of about 4 feet, use the boathook. To prevent a line from falling off the end of the boathook or out of the crook, tape the end to the boathook with some insulating tape.

Once the loop or line is on the cleat, pull the boathook back sharply to break the tape. Once round with the tape will do. If you tape the boathook too well you may not be able to break it free, but this doesn't really matter as you will be attached to the shore and can free the boathook later. You could also use cotton wrapped round a few times rather than tape. Using the boathook to offer up lines to the shore from high-topsided boats is especially handy.

HOW TO HOOK A CLEAT

■ Fit the line into the crook of the boathook and hold this tight.

■ Then as you offer the line up to the cleat, allow a little slack.

■ Thread the line on to the cleat.

■ And withdraw the boathook.

The crew on the bow can tell the helm where the buoy is by pointing the boathook at it

Boathook attached to the boat by rustler's hitches with enough line to use the boathook from stem to stern

We also use the boathook as a method of communication. If we are short-handed and we are picking up a mooring buoy, the crew on the bow can tell the helm where the buoy is by pointing the boathook obviously and directly at it. As the boat approaches and the helm loses sight of the buoy, he or she has a very good idea of where it is by watching the boathook.

For extendible boathooks, it is important to make sure that they will extend quickly and that they have not seized. Sailing back to the man overboard, grabbing the boathook and finding we cannot reach more than a few feet with it will be disappointing to say the least. A little silicone will do the trick to ensure that the hook will extend nicely. That's the boathook prepared.

Of course the minute we get the boathook out we need to ready a slip knot, so that when it goes over the side and heads out to sea we can chase after it and retrieve it on board. Or, better still, we could tie a line from the boat to the boathook with rustler's hitches at either end so that the boathook would be attached to the boat if it went over and we could release it in an emergency. And, finally, the boathook needs to be to hand.

Boathook in the drink but not lost

SHARING A CLEAT

A standard Walcon cleat offers three places to which to attach a line: either of the uprights or the horizontal. So if we want to add in a bow restrainer we add it into one side of the cleat to allow others to share the cleat.

SHORE LINES

If you are running a line ashore when rafted up and you see a cleat awash with other lines, then tie a bowline into your line and feed it under everyone else's and over the top of the cleat. Now they can release your line to get theirs out and then put your line back when they have gone. In fact, each line can be removed independently. Mind you if you are outboard of them in the raft and they are leaving, you will be involved one way or another in helping them.

How to share a Walcon cleat when using a bow restrainer

How not to share a Walcon cleat

⌘ Sometimes you'll have to find space for your shore line on a busy cleat like this.

⌘ Tie a bowline into the end of your shore line and feed it under everyone else's and over the top of the cleat.

⌘ If your shore line is attached like this others in the raft can easily release it to get their lines out.

SHOES

Visiting crew ask quite sensibly: 'What shoes should I wear?' Shoes that don't come off, preferably. Anything flat. Of course, I started out with sprauncy deck shoes, then graduated to performance sailing shoes, because they laced up and didn't slip off. Then I moved into everyday lace-ups which have as much grip about the deck as any deck shoe or specialist sailing shoe I have ever worn and the soles don't seem to perish as quickly as some of the sailing brands. Oxidised soles can be lethal. The point is that it doesn't matter what one wears. One's best grip on deck probably comes from bare feet. When wet and cold, a good pair of sea boots is essential.

TOP TIP

Wipe a little polish over leather laces before tying them. This helps them to grip nicely and makes sure they stay done up.

TOP TIP

Laces that won't come undone

If you ever have trouble with laces coming undone try tying them like this. Cross the laces over not once but twice to hold this part in place and stop it slipping. Now, just like tying a reef knot, take the left-hand bight behind and through the right-hand bight. Then the right-hand bight behind and through the left-hand bight and tighten. It undoes by pulling one end of one shoe lace but will stay done up all day long. This method of tying laces works well with leather laces.

 Scan this QR code to watch a video on this method of tying shoe laces.

TOP TIP

Walk about the boat like a cat. Anyone who stomps around a boat and makes a massive bang as they land in the cockpit really has very little sympathy for the boat or anyone below. No noise. That's the seamanlike way.

KEEP A CLEAN HEAD

A smelly head makes the difference between a boat I want to sail on and a boat I want to get off. The way I keep my head smelling sweet is to run it dry bowl with no additives. I shower in my head and so clean the bowl and surrounding areas with a normal bathroom cleaner each time.

Some who operate the dry bowl system say that they get a nasty smell the first time they pump anything through. This will be anaerobic water that has been sitting in the inlet pipe. I don't get this, but if you do then before leaving the boat shut the inlet valve and pump the water into the bowl to remove it from the pipe and then pump the bowl dry. With no water on the inlet side you should prevent this smell.

After time the piping can begin to smell and that's the time to replace it.

If you have sworn by a little something down the loo and decided to move over to nothing you will find that the pump and system will squeak a bit in protest at the lack of its daily fix of whatever but very shortly will settle down and function wonderfully sans olive oil, silicone or WD40 or whatever patent additive we used to give it.

Holding tanks? I do not want to carry my ordure around with me so I don't have one, but if you are in the Med, a locked-in marina or on inland waterways you will have to have one. Soon the bureaucrats will insist that all of us have to have one, but as I have a tidal berth with an average range of three metres, which sweeps everything clean twice a day I don't think I need a holding tank. In any event when we are on the berth all crew must use the marina facilities.

GLOSSARY

Back spring (aft spring, stern spring)	Stops the stern moving backwards
Belay	To tie off, secure
Bight	A U-shaped curve in a rope
End for end	To turn a boat in her berth or on a pontoon using warps so she is facing the other way. Also to turn a sheet or halyard around so that the ends are exchanged
Head spring (forward spring, bow spring)	Stops the bow moving forward
Loop	A fold or doubling of the rope through which another rope can be passed to form a knot or hitch
Make fast	To tie off, secure
Standing end	The end of the rope not involved in making the knot, eg the end attached to the fender
Standing part	The section between the knot and the standing end
Warp (noun)	A rope used for manhandling a vessel or securing a vessel alongside a quay or jetty for mooring, or a rope attached to the anchor
Warp (verb)	To move the boat around using warps/rope
Winding her in her berth	To turn a boat in her berth or on a pontoon using warps so she is facing the other way
Working end/running end	The active end of the rope involved in making the knot
Working part	The section between the knot and the working end/running end

GETTING OFF THE BERTH

This is the one thing that everyone, me included, finds the most stressful. I will have fretted over the forecast wind strength and direction, the tides and so forth before I left home. Then as I near the boat I will be looking at the trees and flags to see what we really have. Will the wind be kind to me? Or will it drive me in the direction of my neighbour as I leave. I will have worked out precisely what the tide is doing at my berth before I arrive and I will have timed my departure from the dock to use the tide to my advantage.

It is the wind strength at the moment of departure that I cannot be absolutely sure about. I will have a good idea, of course. And even if I have 20 knots of wind blowing me into trouble, there is every chance that there will be the occasional lull. I watch for the lulls and then grab my chance.

So step 1 of getting off the berth is about reading the conditions, establishing what they will do to you. What will happen to us when we let go of the string?

CONDITIONS: WIND AND TIDE

We arrive at our boat. Check the wind strength and direction, on the instruments and at the top of the mast. It's worth checking the wind speed and direction on deck, too. The anemometer on top of the mast may well be reading a higher wind speed and it is on deck that will affect us most. If you are unsure of the wind direction, just see which way the seagulls are facing when they perch on posts. They will always be facing into the wind.

A glance over the side will confirm what we expected the tide to be doing. Checking the lines will reveal which ones are doing any work. Any slack line is not in play. We could get rid of it and the boat would stay exactly where she is, held in place by the active lines. If our berth lies fore and aft with the tide and most do, then

> ### Calculate the speed of the tide by eye *i*
>
> We can get a rough idea of a boat's speed through the water by dropping something biodegradable that won't sink immediately in at the bow and counting how many seconds it takes to reach the stern. Now the length of the boat in feet x 3 divided by the seconds x 5 will give you the speed in knots:
>
> So boat length 35 feet x 3 = 105 ÷ time taken for the last of my bread roll to go from the bow to the stern
>
> 4 sec x 5 = 20 gives a boat speed of just over 5 knots
>
> To calculate the speed of the tide we do the same. We probably don't need a bread roll as twigs and general detritus pass through my berth all the time. You can even use bubbles. Time how long they take to go from the bow to the stern. If this is 20 seconds, for a 35-foot boat the speed of the tide is 1 knot; if it is 10 seconds it is 2 knots. This is all part of the preparation. Now we know the exact speed of the tide that will affect us.

generally only one spring line will be under tension at any one time; the one holding us against the tide, or if there is no tide, against the wind. The other will be slack. Head spring tight? Then the back spring will be slack. I say generally because it is possible to have the tide pushing through the berth in one direction and the wind pushing through the berth in the other direction and they can even each other out, so neither spring has any tension in it. Or at slack water with no breeze both springs can be slack. But that is good news generally because it means that when we let go, our boat isn't going to go anywhere. In any case, we can see from the mooring warps what will happen when we let go.

The next thing to consider is how our boat will behave under engine and how she will be affected by the wind when under way. Does the bow blow off easily? Left to their own devices, all boats will lie bow downwind with the wind on the quarter or thereabouts. When driving astern, again the stern of all boats will find the wind. Prior to getting way on when driving astern though we have to consider another factor.

PROP WALK

All boats with one propeller experience prop walk. When you put the gear lever into ahead there will be some prop walk. Generally this will barely be noticeable. When you put the gear into astern, however, prop walk can become much more noticeable. I say 'can' because there are some boats that experience very little prop walk when going astern and these are the ones that are as easy to drive astern as they are to drive forward. They tend to be the more modern, racy boats with bulb keels and sail drives. At the other end of the scale a long keel, heavy displacement boat will have a great deal of prop walk to contend with. What is happening is that the propeller walks the stern in the direction it is turning before the boat gathers any way and so the boat goes sideways first. With some way on, the rudder comes into play. The diagram above right shows what the wind and tide do to my boat when driving astern.

Which way will your boat kick when going astern? Left-handed props rotate anti-clockwise when going ahead and clockwise when going astern, so they will wind the boat to starboard when in astern. Right-handed props do the opposite. In astern they will wind the boat to port. But how do we know which we have? Make sure the boat is attached securely to the dock, the back spring is secure and then put her into astern. Look over the side. On one side there will be turbulence and on the other the water will be calm. She will walk in the direction of the calm water.

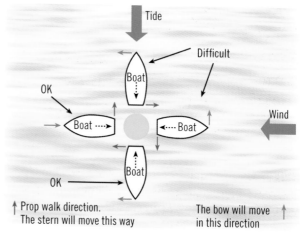

↑ Prop walk direction. The stern will move this way

The bow will move in this direction ↑

Starboard prop walk astern

Crash turn

Having prop walk means that a boat will favour a turn in one direction. Prop walk astern to starboard? Then our tight turn will be to port. We will use this to turn the boat in her own length, more or less. We will start the turn from stationary with the helm hard aport and give a blast of ahead. This will bounce off the rudder and start the bow moving to port. We want to give just enough thrust to get the bow moving but not so much that we get any way on or start moving forward. Then we give a blast of astern and this keeps the bow moving to port as the stern walks to starboard. We keep doing this until we are facing the other way. If we tried the turn in the opposite direction we would simply go sideways.

So boats who kick to starboard astern will have their crash turn to port and those that kick to port astern will have their crash turn to starboard. This crash turn is what we call our 'get out of jail free card'. It gets us out of scrapes. All boats with a central rudder and a keel will do it. Long keelers just take rather more bursts of ahead and astern to get round. I have heard mixed reports about bilge keelers. Some, like the Sadler 29, behave just like a fin keel boat, others are less helpful. Whatever you have you need to test her out and see what she will do for you.

 Scan this QR code to watch a video on the 180° turn.

FENDERING

So now we are armed with information – 'prepared' – we had better fender up well. Fenders go between us and what we might hit so they need to be in the right place at the right height. If we are moored to a pontoon and we set them too high they can pop out. Set them too low and any wind that heels the boat can drop the fender below the pontoon. We may be on a finger berth and may have a neighbour, so we need to set fenders to pontoon height on one side and at gunwhale height on the other, just in case we come to rest on our neighbour or he does the same to us.

Whenever I arrive at a port or marina where I don't know if I will be alongside a pontoon or rafted up, I set three fenders either side for a pontoon and can have them at gunwhale height in a flash if I am to raft up. I also set bow and stern lines on port and starboard.

The fenders are at pontoon height on one side and gunwhale height on the other

FENDERS FROM PONTOON HEIGHT TO GUNWHALE HEIGHT IN AN INSTANT

■ A fender down to the water and up a bit is generally right for most pontoons.

■ This becomes, on a 35-foot boat (in fact on most sailing boats), a fender set at gunwhale height for rafting up or as protection from another boat coming alongside when you take it under the lower guardrail and over the upper one.

Fender attached with a slip clove hitch

Fender attached at the base of a stanchion using a round turn and two half hitches

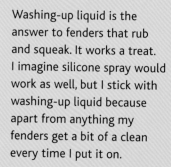
The two knots I use for fenders are the clove hitch and the round turn and two half hitches. And I tie them close to the stanchion to prevent them sliding along the guard wire and out of position when either leaving or arriving at the berth. I use a slip clove hitch which is easy to pull apart for adjustment when coming onto and off a berth.

I would then use the round turn and two half hitches if there was a lot of movement in the marina and the fenders were getting a bit of a workout against the dock or another boat. And I will tie this at the base of the stanchion. The idea of this is that with the running end being under the knot and held in place by the weight of the hanging fender it is unlikely to come undone.

As a general point it is very worthwhile, unless one is fabulously wealthy, to tie the fenders on with a knot that will not give way. I have known many who have eschewed the humble clove hitch in favour of something much more glamorous when tying their fenders on and they have all managed to lose fenders as the knots unravelled and the fenders dropped off. For some reason they never seem to make the link between an unconventional and ineffective knot and the loss of the fender. I have seen fenders tied on with a cow hitch and as long one is certain that the type of line used will not slip against the guardrail or wire that is fine. If in doubt, stick to the accepted norm of clove hitch or round turn and two half hitches.

And finally on fenders, we need to think ahead where we will need them. When sharing a finger berth with a neighbour it is always a good idea to have a couple of fenders set on their side at gunwhale height when leaving or returning.

I stow my fenders 'inside' the back rail of the pushpit when under way. I have never lost a fender

I do think this type of fender stowage is asking for trouble. But then who am I to tell people how to spend their money

BACK-UP PLAN

We also need to have a back-up plan in case anything goes wrong. Missing our berth and arriving alongside our neighbour is more likely to happen when we return to the berth, rather than when we leave. And in any event the techniques for getting off in the next chapter will prevent us running into our neighbour.

If we have been blown on to our neighbour while we were either exiting or returning to the berth and the tide is running us out of our berth, then we need to attach a midships line between us and our neighbour quickly, to stop us scraping down his side as the tide pushes us back. Then it is a question of fendering up anything that might come into contact with the dock or neighbour and getting a line ashore on to a cleat at the front of our berth. Release the midship line holding you to your neighbour and hang off the line attached to the front of the berth. Now we just need to warp her back to her berth.

⌘ Get a midships line across to your neighbour now.

⌘ Then fender up anything that might come into contact with the dock or neighbour.

⌘ And get a line ashore on to a cleat at the front of your berth.

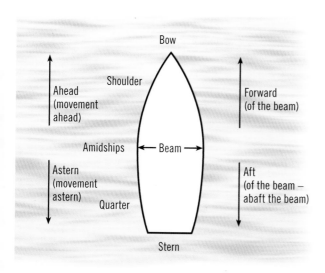

Parts of the boat

GRIP

Part of our preparation is establishing how much grip we will have on the water. As long as we have water travelling along the hull and over the rudder, we have grip. Say we have 1 knot of tide. If we motor into this 1 knot at a speed through the water (our boat speed) of 2 knots we will have a speed of water over the hull of 2 knots and therefore a grip on the water of 2 knots and yet a speed over the ground of just 1 knot, because we are being pushed back by the 1 knot of tide.

We are in control. However, if we go with the tide at a boat speed of 2 knots, we will again have a speed of water over the hull of 2 knots, but we will be travelling over the ground at 3 knots – our 2 knots through the water plus 1 knot of tide and we will be out of control. And this, of course, is why we always, always, always moor into the tide. Some people seem to think they can get away with mooring with the tide, but the tide always teaches you an embarrassing lesson.

Now before we look at the range of different conditions for departure that we are likely to come across, we need to prepare. We are going to be using bridles (string that goes round things), springs (string that uses angles to hold you on or lever you off) and slipped lines (string that goes from ship to shore and back and can be released from onboard).

We are going to control these from the cockpit. As we want the lines to slip, so we should choose a type of line that will slip easily. Most line will be fine, but do not expect a chewed-up old three-strand line to slip as well as a nice new and shiny polyester braid. I have used a Dyneema core with a red and yellow polyester braid outer for most of the shots because it shows up well and it slips against itself nicely. That said, we also used other three-strand and braided ropes and we led the lines through fairleads, D rings, around stanchion posts, blocks on toe rails and a whole variety of turning devices and never a snag. So perhaps I am being over cautious by suggesting we

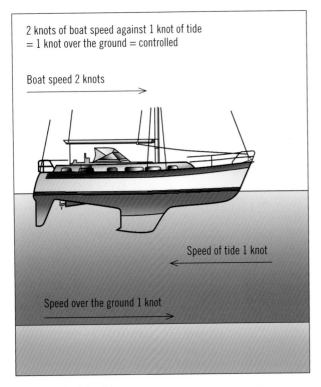

2 knots of boat speed against 1 knot of tide
= 1 knot over the ground = controlled

Boat speed 2 knots

Speed of tide 1 knot

Speed over the ground 1 knot

Going against the tide

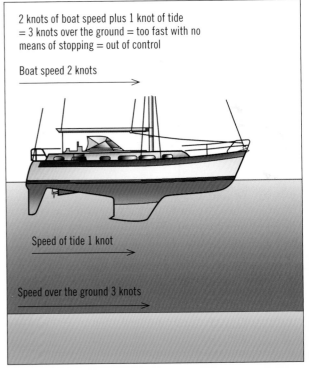

2 knots of boat speed plus 1 knot of tide
= 3 knots over the ground = too fast with no means of stopping = out of control

Boat speed 2 knots

Speed of tide 1 knot

Speed over the ground 3 knots

Going with the tide

need a smooth-running rope for our slipped line. Still, better safe than sorry.

Now, before you festoon the boat with all sorts of line to assist your departure, do check that the conditions really are going to move the boat away from the dock so fast that you could not release the lines from the shore, step aboard and drive off the berth. I find I am often able to do this.

Assuming we are not, then we have a variety of ways in which we might be moored and a variety of techniques for exiting in various conditions. I have generalised wind strengths as light (up to 5 knots), moderate (5–15 knots), stronger (15–25 knots). Any wind stronger than 25 knots trying to blow us off the pontoon is going to make things pretty tricky. So let's wait until it calms down a bit.

Different boats experience different windage. A high topsided modern boat is going to be blown about by the wind more than a classic displacement boat with low topsides and a long keel. And wind angle to the boat is key. Wind on the beam will push the boat around more than wind on the bow or stern.

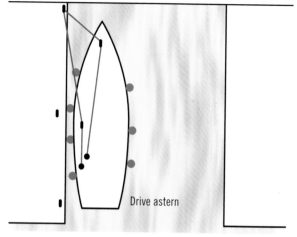

Using a bridle

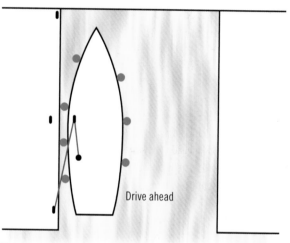

Using a spring

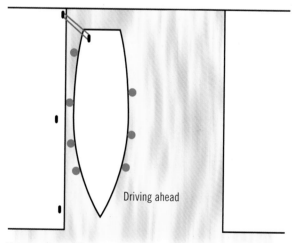

Using a slipped line

TOP TIP

Diesel engines like to be put under load, so if you're running the engine while alongside for any time, put it into gear. Leaving it in neutral will glaze the cylinders over time.

FINGER BERTH, BOWS IN

Tide on the bow or stern, wind light to moderate, blowing the boat on or off

Technique 1: slipped bow bridle

To control this from the cockpit we would set a slipped bow bridle and drive astern against this. To set this up, attach the inboard end to a secure point in the cockpit or a stern cleat. Run the line along the deck inside the shrouds to the bow, round the bow cleat, round the cleat on the dock and back on board amidships. Secure on a winch. Put her in gear astern and check she is holding alongside nicely before removing the bow, stern lines and springs. If she starts to wander off the dock, increase the revs and this will bring her back. To depart, we leave the engine clicked into astern, take the line off the winch and haul in steadily on the inboard end.

The bow bridle works for everybody. You might be concerned about having a length of line that could fall into the water. Let me assure you that first it is not going to be long enough to come close to any prop or stern gear, second that as we haul it in we are shortening the length of line, third that we have run the inboard end of the line inside the shrouds specifically to make sure that there can be no chance of this line going over the side and into the water and fourth we are going astern and therefore distancing our 'delicate' bits from the line as we do so.

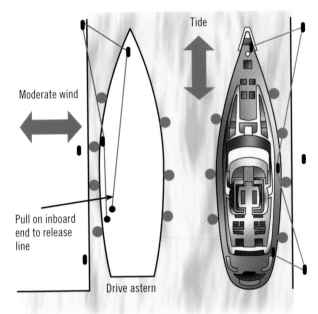

Tide

Moderate wind

Pull on inboard end to release line

Drive astern

Driving astern against a slipped bow bridle

As long as we do not have the tide or wind pushing us through the berth we can always put the engine into neutral before hauling in the line. I prefer to leave the engine in astern to make sure my bow doesn't blow into my neighbour. After all, I will only be using this system if the boat, left unattended, would drift or be blown off the dock. With all these things you need to experiment and see what works best for you.

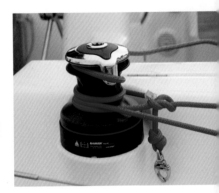

⌘ Here we are using a spinnaker halyard for the bridle, snap shackle end inboard.

⌘ The inboard end of this bow bridle is attached to the stern cleat.

⌘ With no immediate strong point in the cockpit or cleats, *Layla Ann* has used a winch for the inboard and the outboard end of the bridle.

SLIPPED BOW BRIDLE STEP BY STEP

■ Run the line along the deck inside the shrouds to the bow, round the bow cleat, round the cleat on the dock and back on board amidships.

■ Secure on a winch.

■ Put her in gear astern and check she is holding alongside nicely before removing the bow and stern lines and springs

■ If she starts to wander off the dock, increase the revs and this will bring her back.

■ Leave the engine clicked into astern, ready to go.

■ Take the bridle off the winch and haul on the inboard end.

■ Free! Note the line going inside the shrouds to avoid any contact with the prop.

■ And we're off.

▲ *Slipped bow bridle on* Quintessence, *a Bavaria 42*

◄ *Slipped bow bridle on* Layla Ann, *a Dufour 375*

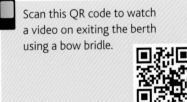

Scan this QR code to watch a video on exiting the berth using a bow bridle.

Technique 2: slipped midship spring

SETTING UP A SLIPPED MIDSHIP SPRING

■ Secure the inboard end to a strong point in the cockpit or a stern cleat.

■ The return line from the shore cleat is led through the centre of the cleat to reduce friction when we haul in.

■ Take the line up to and around the forward end of the midship cleat.

■ Then round the cleat by the stern on shore and back up to the cockpit and secure on a winch.

■ Adjust the line to make sure you have the least amount of line to slip. The fixed end should be on the cleat and the free end on the winch.

■ Put the engine into ahead. Now, with the boat holding alongside, you can remove the springs, bow and stern lines. To leave, put the engine into neutral, take the slipped spring line off the winch and haul in on the inboard end.

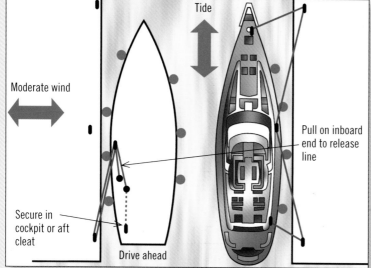

Tide

Moderate wind

Pull on inboard end to release line

Secure in cockpit or aft cleat

Drive ahead

◀ Driving ahead against a slipped midship spring

Technique 3: fixed midship spring

Instead of a slipped spring line we could use a fixed spring line which we would need to lift off the cleat before departing.

Then we set up the spring from the cleat on shore through the centre of the midship cleat and up to a cockpit winch. To depart put the engine into neutral, take the inboard end off the winch to give you some slack, lift the plastic loop of the spring off the cleat and bring it on board. Put the engine astern and exit the berth. If you have high topsides you can either lift the plastic loop off with a boathook or attach another light line to the plastic loop and use this to lift the spring off the cleat.

The boat should be lying alongside nicely and by adjusting the helm you should be able to keep her straight. But every boat is different; different keel configurations, different propulsion methods from sail drive to shaft, different positions of midship cleats and so forth. And some boats have a tendency to tuck their bow in, which, of course, kicks their stern out. The modern Dufour did this as did the classic Rustler and the Contessa. The way round this is to attach another line to the plastic hoop of the spring and lead this back on board through the centre of the aft cleat or fairlead to keep it in place.

No midship cleat? Here Quintessence *uses a U-bolt as a midship point*

It helps when getting a spring on and off a cleat to keep the line slightly open so we use a piece of plastic tubing over the line. This plastic tubing also protects the line and adds to its durability

⌘ No midships cleat? Then use a block on the genoa track.

⌘ Another midship cleat alternative: a snapshackle attached to the bottom of a stanchion.

Yes, a stanchion. We are not aiming to put a great strain on this line and the base of most stanchions should be up to the job. If you feel your stanchions are too fragile for this, then fair enough. Remember that there is a stout post coming out of the toe rail over which the stanchion slots. So the base is a bit more solid than it looks.

Setting up a fixed midship spring: from the cleat on shore through the centre of the midship cleat and up to a cockpit winch

Look, Mum, no hands!

This 'stern' line will hold the boat nicely alongside if she decides to kick her stern out. To leave, put the engine in neutral which will stop her trying to turn her bow in and remove the plastic loop of the spring – only now you have some assistance as you can use the extra 'stern' line to help you get the hoop off the cleat.

The same applies if you found that the stern was kicking out when lying to a slipped midship spring: you would add in a slipped retaining line for your stern.

It is worth suggesting that setting up and testing all these manoeuvres should be tried out on a wet Wednesday afternoon when no one is around and with your boat well fendered up. And don't remove the bow, stern and spring lines until the new system is clearly holding the boat nicely alongside the dock.

If the wind is blowing you on quite strongly you might want to wind the boat as far out of the berth as possible. Set up your fixed midship spring and then by clicking the boat in and out of gear and shortening the length of the spring by winching it in, wind yourself out of the berth.

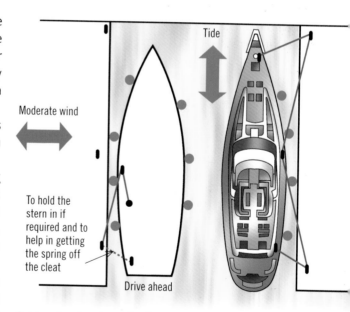

Driving ahead against a fixed midship spring

Southern Cross *holding her stern in with a 'stern' line attached to the plastic loop of the spring line*

Layla Ann *with her high topsides uses the 'stern' line to get the spring off the cleat as she leaves her berth*

Slipped 'stern' line added into the slipped midship spring

Half out of the berth

Technique 4: slipped midship line

This will hold the boat in most wind and tide conditions. We don't use any engine for this; it is simply the line that holds us. The bow cannot wander very far off the dock because as it does, it digs the stern into the dock. The same applies to the stern. The boat cannot move forward or back against the dock. It is a lovely way of attaching the boat. For a smooth single-handed departure set this midship line to slip.

Whenever using the midship cleat for any slipped line I always have the inbound part of the line, the part I am hauling on, around the front of the midship cleat and the outbound part of the line through the centre of the midship cleat. It's just habit and with a loose line feeding its way through the centre of the midship cleat I feel this is less likely to snag, slip off or end up in the drink. Again, you need to experiment and see what suits you best.

⌘ Midship line rigged as a slip.

⌘ With the inboard end secure in the cockpit, run the line out to the midship cleat to the dock and back, and secure on a cockpit winch.

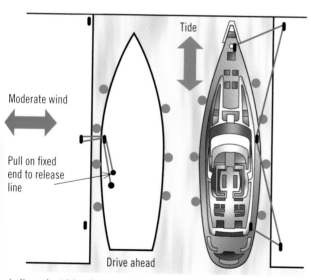

A slipped midship line

⌘ Go out round the forward end of the midship cleat and back through the centre of it to keep these two parts of the line separate so they don't rub against each other when you haul in.

FINGER BERTH, STERN IN

Tide on the bow or stern, wind light to moderate, blowing the boat on or off

Technique 5: slipped stern line

This is a very useful and simple slipped line technique. Even if the wind is blowing you quite strongly off the dock it should be possible to hold the boat alongside. A few extra revs should do the trick. On a day with a fairly gentle breeze, try putting the gear into neutral and see how quickly you move away from the dock. Then put the engine into ahead and see how the boat brings herself alongside. When you are ready to go, skip the line and drive off.

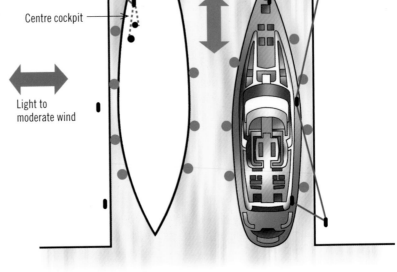

Driving the boat against a slipped stern line

Wind moderate or stronger blowing the boat off

Technique 6: slipped stern bridle

If you were being blown off the dock you could use a slipped stern bridle, running from a secure point in the cockpit to your midship cleat, down to the stern cleat ashore, back on board via your stern cleat and up to a cockpit winch. This will help to hold you alongside and keep the bow from being blown off.

You can always warp the boat along the dock so that she is half out of her berth and set up a slipped midship spring or, indeed, a fixed midship spring and drive against this.

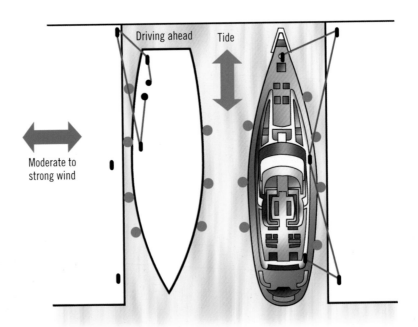

Driving ahead against a slipped stern bridle

SETTING UP A SLIPPED STERN LINE

■ Make one end fast in the cockpit. You can use a secure point for this.

■ Or you can make a bight in the rope and loop this over a winch. Here, a bight was made by tying an alpine butterfly knot into the middle of the line. (I use an alpine butterfly knot because I want to tie a bight in the middle of the rope so that I have as little line to slip as possible – see Chapter 7 for how to tie this.)

■ Run the line out through the centre of the aft cleat, round the shore cleat, back around the end of the aft cleat and secure on the winch. Put the engine into ahead and take off the rest of the lines. When you are ready to go, put the engine into neutral for a moment, release the end of the line to be slipped and haul in on the inboard end.

■ Again, the two parts of the line are kept apart.

■ I am also quite happy to use one winch for both the fixed end of the line and the free end of the line.

■ Sometimes we have to be inventive. Here, *Southern Cross* is using a couple of winches.

■ See how little line there is to trail in the water. Not enough to get into any trouble.

■ And away we go with a fender trying to escape.

ALONG A LONG PONTOON, WITH BOATS AHEAD AND ASTERN

You can use a midship slipped line to hold you on to the pontoon or a midship spring or a slipped bow bridle or you could drive ahead against a slipped stern line or a stern bridle. It all depends on how much room you have and what the wind and tide are doing. If you are being blown off the pontoon and you are heading into the tide then any of the techniques will work fine. When you release the line you will start to be blown off the pontoon, the bow will be caught by the tide and you drive off. If the tide is on your stern or if you are being blown on then you will need to spring off the pontoon.

Tide on the bow or beam on, wind blowing on

Technique 7: spring out the bow and drive ahead

Use a slipped stern spring with the fixed and slipped ends secured in the cockpit and led to your stern cleat and then to a cleat amidships on shore and back. If you drive astern against this, the bow will come out.

Make sure you fender up the aft end of the boat well. The further out you take the bow the more protection our stern will need. Also part of the preparation is to fender up the side opposite the pontoon to gunwhale height in case the tide catches your bow and for some reason you are unable to release the spring line and the tide swings you around into the boat behind. Fenders at gunwhale height should afford some protection against this.

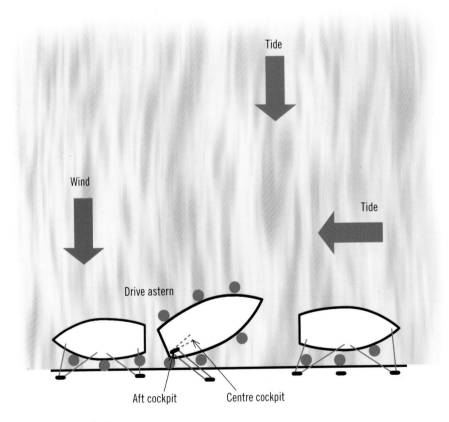

Springing out the bow

Tide on the stern, boat being blown on

Technique 8: spring out the stern and drive astern

If you have the tide astern and are being blown on you need to get the stern out into the tide and drive out backwards just to give you some room to manoeuvre. Having got out into the fairway or river you should have enough space to turn the boat in her own length if need be so that you are facing in the correct direction.

Of course, there should be no surprises about whether you will have the tide on the bow or the stern when the time comes to leave. You will have come in and berthed bows into the tide. And so when you leave you need to leave bows into the tide or at slack water. But if you really have to leave with the tide on your stern and the boat

being blown on, then you can spring the stern out. If you are being blown off the pontoon then again you want to get the stern out into the tide, but getting the stern out will be easier as the wind will be helping you.

Use a slipped bow spring with the fixed and slipped ends secured in the cockpit. The line is then led to the bow (inside the shrouds), round your bow cleat, down to a cleat on shore amidships and back to the bow and to the cockpit. Then with the bow well fendered, drive ahead against this and spring out the stern. When the stern is out into the tide, put the engine into neutral and take the slipped line off the winch and haul in on the standing end.

Again, as with springing out the bow, fender up the side opposite the pontoon to gunwhale height in case the tide swings your stern round and you end up lying alongside the boat ahead.

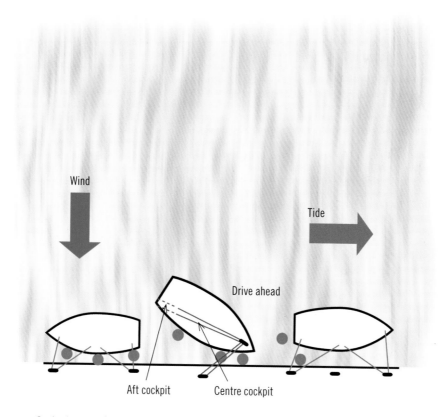

Wind

Tide

Drive ahead

Aft cockpit

Centre cockpit

Springing out the stern

Tide on the beam, boat being blown on

Technique 9: drive ahead against a slipped line from your far quarter

If you are being blown on and the tide is pushing you on to the pontoon you can either spring the bow out as described in Technique 8, or there is another technique worth looking at. Again, you can set this as a slipped line. Take a line from your outboard aft cleat to a cleat on the dock and back. Then drive ahead against this. You will need to fender up your quarter and stern very well as the quarter and stern of the boat will be rotated against the dock. But doing this will enable you to get your bow out and the boat lying at 90° to the dock. With the bow now pointing into wind and tide, release the slipped line and motor off.

SUMMARY

All the systems worked on all the boats – long fin /skeg and shaft, medium fin/blade and shaft, bulb keel /blade and sail drive and long keel – but we needed to adjust line lengths and find the right balance, each time. So they should work fine on your boat. It is just a question of experimenting and finding the technique that works best for you. Whenever you try out a technique for the first time do fender up well, have extra lines attached to make sure you don't 'lose' the boat and only take off all lines when you know that your new technique is working and holding the boat and you have tested less and more engine throttle and have found the balance.

My favourite technique when I am bows in is the bow bridle. This is so easy to manage single-handed from the cockpit, even if we are using a slipped stern line to hold us alongside because of the wind. If I am stern in then the slipped stern line is my favourite. I will upgrade it to a stern bridle if the wind is trying to blow us off the dock, because being attached amidships the stern bridle will hold the boat alongside better than the slipped stern line.

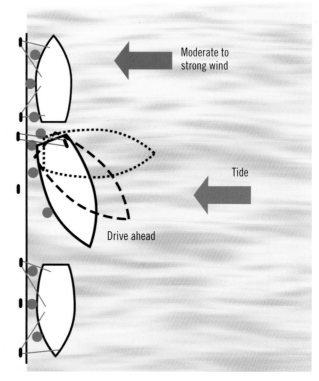

Springing the bow out with a slipped line to an outboard cleat

TOP TIP

When racing, yachts will not wear an ensign. The crew will raise the ensign when they finish.

I love the fact that I am allowed to fly the Red Ensign, to demonstrate my nationality. That makes me feel proud and I treat this privilege responsibly

Dorothy Lee *driving ahead against a slipped line from her far quarter. We had a preventer on the bow to stop her going too far, seeing as how I was on the dock taking the picture*

GETTING ONTO THE BERTH

So now we are off the dock, how are we going to get back on? There are a number of systems we can use. All we have to do is a get a line to the dock and around a cleat which we can drive against in one way or another. First though we need to consider our approach.

THE APPROACH

We will always moor into the tide. Whether we are coming alongside a stretch of pontoon or into a dead end finger berth, rafting up alongside or coming up to a mooring buoy, we will always drive into the tide. If we are berthing 'bows in' we drive ahead into the tide and if we are to be 'stern in' we drive astern into the tide. The tide will usually be the dominant force on the boat.

Occasionally in a strong wind and slack water, the wind will be the stronger force, but a quite modest rate of the tide will usually overpower the effect of the wind, but not always, so we need to judge which is having the greater effect on the boat. I have a berth where the prevailing wind blows through and has a significant effect on the boat and requires quite a strong tide to overcome it.

We also need to consider the effect of a crosswind. As long as we have some way on and a grip on the water we should be able to counter any crosswind, although our ability to do this will depend on our displacement and the profile we present to the wind. Modern light displacement boats with high topsides are very susceptible to windage, older heavy displacement long keelers are less so. In a modern boat with a crosswind you cannot afford to be too tentative. She will be swept sideways quite quickly so a positive approach to the berth will be required. Being light, modern boats can usually stop very quickly and a quick burst of astern should stop any forward movement.

If you are mooring in a crosswind you will need to allow for this. In case you're being blown on to the berth, aim high, to windward, and use the wind to blow you into your berth. If you've misjudged and are a little to windward of the berth, then it is just a matter of waiting as the wind blows you on. The one thing you don't want to do is aim at your berth as the wind will blow you off course and very likely T-bone you on the end of the finger.

If you are being blown away from your berth, you could again aim high, to windward, and allow the wind to blow you into the gap, although doing this you risk being blown on to your neighbour or being blown past the berth and having to bail out of the exercise... It's preferable to approach the berth at an angle, to go past and turn back up into the wind and drive in. Then you have control.

You will also want to moor on the side to which you kick in astern, assuming you are mooring bows in. Or if you are mooring stern to, then you will want to moor on the side to which you kick in ahead. So that when you bring the boat to a stop she tucks herself into the dock.

The following techniques are designed to be handled by one person from the cockpit or the side deck by the cockpit of the boat. Don't step off the boat until she is stationary and holding alongside.

If you are short-handed (you and one crew) then one person can man the helm while the other does the rope work. Most important here is to remember that the helmsman should never leave the helm. If the crew has missed when they tried to get a line ashore or something has gone wrong there is the temptation to leave the helm and help. Now what you have is a boat that is not attached to the shore and not being controlled by the helm; this is highly undesirable. As frustrating as it might be, the helmsman must remain at the helm and control the boat until the crew is ready to try again.

The beauty with all the techniques that follow is that the risk of 'missing' has been reduced and because you will prepare and practise, you will always get that cleat first time, every time. Well, that's the theory, anyway.

▶ Angle of approach for wind blowing us off the berth, although the wind here was very light

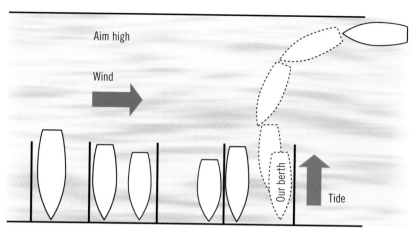

Aim high when the wind is blowing you on

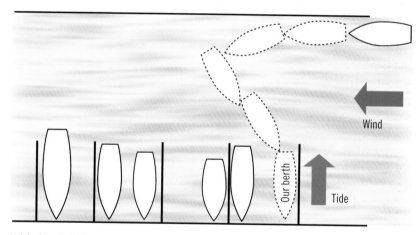

With the wind blowing you off the berth, turn into wind on your approach

FERRY GLIDING

You can also use the tide to help you moor and make the boat move sideways. This technique is used by everyone from large passenger ships to small canoes and kayaks. Let us say you have a tide of 1 knot on the bow. You can hold the boat stationary over the ground by driving into the tide at 1 knot: You will have a boat speed taking you forward through the water of 1 knot so, with the tide running at 1 knot in the opposite direction, you will actually be stationary. Now you want to go sideways so you turn your bow to bring the tide on to one side or the other. The stronger the tide the smaller you make this angle on the bow. As you drive forward, stemming the tide, you will be moved sideways. This is called ferry gliding and sailors use it a great deal.

To use ferry gliding to help you berth, arrive at the pontoon a little way off, turn your bow into the tide, drive against this and get pushed sideways to the pontoon or berth. Just before you arrive, straighten the boat up and come alongside perfectly. Check this out on a wet Wednesday afternoon, in plenty of space and with plenty of fenders.

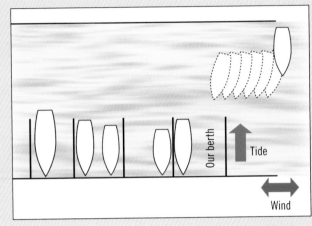

Ferry gliding

■ Giles is ferry gliding *Quintessence* off her berth

■ He continues to ferry glide into the fairway

APPROACHING BOWS FIRST

Stern bridle

This is an excellent technique for mooring up to a pontoon or a finger berth, because even if conditions mean that you are unable to get close to the pontoon you should be able to lasso a cleat. With a few coils of line in each hand, even a fairly weak throw should manage to send the line a good 10 feet. So if you are closer to the pontoon than this, say 6 feet off, you will be able to get that crucial line ashore. And 6 feet off the pontoon is some way off. You would hope to be able to get closer than this. Of course, practising lassoing is key. With the line around a shore cleat, simply drive the boat gently against this to bring her alongside. This is my preferred technique for berthing bows in.

I have tested this technique with boats modern and traditional, from low topsides to high topsides, and it works for everybody, every time.

Remember you are not using this bridle to stop the boat; you should slow the boat to a standstill before lassoing the cleat.

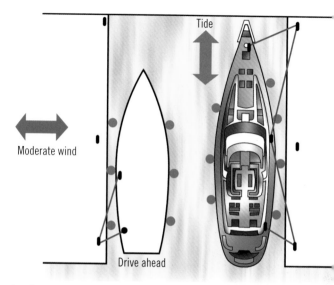

Berthing using a stern bridle

 Scan this QR code to watch a video on getting on to the berth using a stern bridle.

Scan this QR code to watch a video on getting on to the berth using a stern bridle.

TOP TIP

Tie off the boom to the far rail when you are alongside. Saves you banging your head on it every time you go into and out of the cockpit.

The boom is out of harm's way

This is how the stern bridle is set up: a line to the midship cleat led outside everything, brought onboard at the stern cleat and secured on a winch for adjustment

STEP-BY-STEP BERTHING USING A STERN BRIDLE

■ Gather up enough slack in the line to be able to make four coils for the lasso and lay these carefully on the cockpit seating. Check that these are led from outside the guard wire.

■ Spotting the cleat that you aim to lasso, stop the boat and throw the coils on to the pontoon or dock beyond the cleat. Note how far the line goes – it's comfortably past the cleat.

■ Haul in the slack steadily. Click the engine into forward and drive against this bridle. Adjust the engine revs and helm to suit the conditions and hold the boat alongside. Then step off, set the mooring lines and finally knock the engine out of gear and retrieve the bridle.

■ If your finger berth is rather short you may want to set the bridle further forward than the stern cleat. And don't start driving against the bridle until all the slack has been taken in, otherwise you might hit the end!

■ Yellow tape marks that the boat is in the berth as far as she should go. I use this system for returning to my berth every time and so I have marked the line to let me know when my boat is in position.

Springing on using a midship spring

This is the technique I used for years before I moved on to the stern bridle. The midship spring is still an excellent technique, of course, but you do need to be closer to the dock to get the line on than with the stern bridle.

To spring on using a midship spring, you will come back on to a fixed spring that runs from the dock to your midship cleat and back up to a cockpit winch. All you have to do is get that spring on to the first cleat you come to on the finger berth or pontoon. It's always worth making sure that you have led everything the right side of the guard wires. I have often led things the wrong way. I have never actually come to grief, but it has always been a heart-stopping moment to realise that I am trying to hold 8 tonnes of boat on to the dock with a line on the wrong side of the top guard wire that is pressing down on it alarmingly.

It helps to berth on the side to which you kick when in astern if you are coming in bows to. That's worth considering in relation to your own berth and when you are coming into a harbour as a visitor.

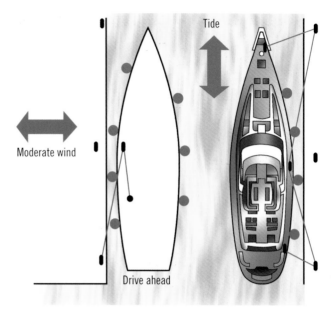

Springing on using a midship spring

⌘ This is how the midship spring is set up.

⌘ Some boats want to tuck their bow in when driving ahead against a midship spring and you can add a 'stern' line to keep you alongside. Just as this line helped to remove the loop when leaving the berth, it can help to get the plastic loop on to the cleat when springing on. This is especially helpful for high topsided boats.

STEP-BY-STEP BERTHING USING A MIDSHIP SPRING

1

■ As you approach the dock, go astern to slow her down and stop her.

2

■ With the gear in neutral, step out of the cockpit.

3

■ And drop the loop over the cleat, return to the cockpit, take up the slack on the winch and then, clicking the engine into ahead, drive against this spring.

4

■ Adjust your position along the dock. Then step down onto the dock, moor up, knock the engine out of gear and remove the spring.

Stern line for arriving at a long pontoon

If there is a stretch of pontoon, you can come alongside using the pre-prepared line with a loop in plastic piping. Secure the line to a stern cleat and drop the loop over a cleat on shore and then drive against this. This will hold the boat in nicely. If the wind is blowing you off with any strength it may be necessary to increase the revs. You can also adjust the angle of the bows a little by introducing some helm or rudder. Steering as if to drive the boat into the pontoon will tuck the bow in and steering as if to drive away from the pontoon will bring the bow out.

Midship line

If conditions are benign you can always arrive alongside a pontoon and from amidships lasso a cleat on shore. With this midship line tight, the boat won't go anywhere, neither forward nor back with any tide nor will she blow off the dock.

Using a stern line to berth at a long pontoon

TOP TIP

Protect your toe rail and teak

Any technique that requires us to drive against a spring or bridle to hold the boat alongside will, over time, introduce chafe in the line or scuffing in a wooden toe rail. Plastic pipe cut lengthways is very useful for protecting narrow teak capping. On wider toe rails use metal strips (strakes) to protect the teak or varnish.

 Scan this QR code to watch a video on springing on with a fixed midship spring.

APPROACHING STERN FIRST

Midship bridle

Many people like to moor stern-to. It is very convenient if you have a gate in the transom and can board over the stern. It's also handy when the finger berth is rather shorter than your boat. You can use a midship bridle for this. To set this up, attach one end of the line to a stern cleat or cockpit winch. Take this outside everything up to the midship cleat, through the centre, then back inboard to the cockpit and secure on a winch. Add in a fender at the stern just for safety. You need to prepare the lasso for this with enough line to make four coils and lay them on the cockpit seating ready to go.

Approach the berth stern first and, as soon as the cockpit is abreast the first cleat you come to on the pontoon and with the boat stationary, step on to the side deck and lasso the cleat. With the line on the dock, haul in on the winch until the line is tight and then drive astern against this. Ease out the line on the winch until

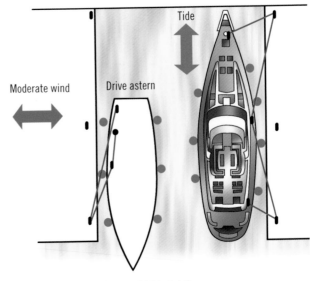

Berthing stern-to using a midship bridle

you are in position. Use engine revs to keep you alongside nicely, to counter any crosswind. Then step off, moor up, knock the engine out of gear and remove the bridle.

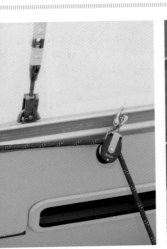

⌘ If you don't have a midship cleat you can use a block shackled onto the toe rail or a block on the genoa sheet lead track.

⌘ I also tie the outboard part of the line that is coming back from the midship cleat on to the upper guard wire with a rustler's hitch. This holds the line in place. After all, I have four coils worth of line lying on the cockpit seating and if that went overboard there is the slight possibility that the loop of line hanging over the side might be able to snag the prop. Unlikely, but I am not going to take the risk. So the rustler's hitch comes to our aid once more.

▲ *If the cleat lies across the pontoon then a midship bridle will work however high our topsides, as the bridle will catch under the wing of the cleat*

▶ *This is how the bridle will be once you have eased yourself into your berth*

Midship bridles do not work for all boats. If your boat has reasonably low topsides everything should be fine. If your boat has high topsides it may not. It also depends on whether or not the end cleat on your finger berth is in line with the pontoon or if it lies across it. Bridles need a degree of lateral element to remain on the cleat. A bow bridle works well because the bow is further from the dock than the beam. The stern too is further from the dock than the beam and so a stern bridle also works well.

You should check the state and mounting of any cleat you are going to use in so far as this is possible (although there's not much one can do when entering a foreign or unfamiliar port or harbour). Again, remember none of these techniques are used for stopping the boat, simply for getting her to come alongside and stay there so we should not be applying any great strain to these cleats.

You can check out if a midship bridle will work for you by setting it up with your mooring warps in place, easing them off so you can drive against the bridle but so that they will hold you if the bridle comes off the cleat. Do be prepared for it to slip off if the cleat is in line with the pontoon and you have a high topsided boat.

Stern first bow bridle

Set the bow bridle the same way as the midship bridle except go from your aft cleat outside everything to the bow cleat and then inboard inside the shrouds to a cockpit winch. You need a long line for this. If you haven't got a long line you can join two lines together. As long as the join is on the inboard side all will be well as the only line that needs to slip past anything is the outboard line going round the cleat on shore. You need to set this up on the dock to check that everything will work well before trying to use it to return to the berth. With the bridle set, take off the other lines to confirm that you are positioned correctly while driving astern and holding to this bow bridle.

As for the midship bridle you will lasso the cleat on shore when it is in line with the cockpit and with the boat stationary. Once the lasso has caught, click the engine into astern and drive back against this bridle until you are in position. Step off, set the mooring lines and then take the engine out of gear.

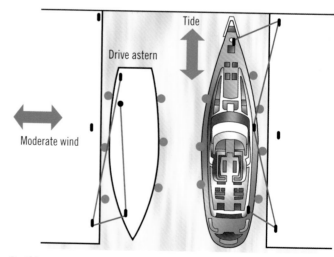

Berthing stern-to using a bow bridle

TRICKY BERTHS, BOWS FIRST

If you have been allocated a berth in between two lots of boats rafted up and there is not much room fore and aft you will have to approach at an angle. You can point your bow or stern into one corner of the berth, get a line on there and drive astern against this. Driving into the tide, aim to get your bow tucked in close behind the boat ahead. Then get a line ashore and then drive astern against this to bring the boat in.

To prepare for this, you will need a long line to run from the cockpit winch, inside the shrouds, to and through the bow cleat nearest to the shore and then outside everything back to us in the cockpit. Tie a bowline in this end. There is very little chance of being able to manage this move single-handed as you need to be at the bow to get the line ashore, but it's possible under benign conditions that allow you to position the boat and then step smartly up to the bow.

The fact that the boats are rafted up three abreast fore and aft of the berth suggests that there are plenty of people around and, as soon as they see you coming, they will be eager to help. If not necessarily out of generosity, certainly out of self interest so that you don't damage their boat. You need to be quite clear about what you would like them to do, because they will not be expecting this. They will expect you to throw them a bow line and a stern line. You could do this, of course, but to be in control your own destiny as far as possible it's better not having people on shore in charge of your lines.

Explain to them: 'I will give you a line with a bowline in it. I would like you to put it on the cleat by the stern of the boat ahead. I will then drive back against this and that will bring my boat alongside.' Add: 'Is that OK?' (meaning do you understand but not saying so in quite such direct terms). Assuming there is agreement, drive into the corner of the berth, step out of the cockpit and hand/throw the line with the bowline in it, to your helper, indicate again the cleat you would like them to put it under so there can be no misunderstanding. As soon as they have attached the line, take up the slack on the winch and click her into astern. You will come into the dock and can lasso a cleat by the stern as you get nearer to the dock if the boat needs a little help.

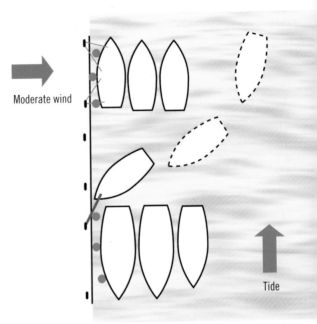

Moderate wind

Tide

▲ *Tricky berth between other boats*

The line is on. Now drive astern against this to bring the boat in

TRICKY BERTHS, STERN FIRST

If your boat is easy to control when going astern you might consider approaching this berth stern-to and mooring stern to the tide.

If you are approaching stern first you may not need assistance from the shore, because you will drive your stern into the corner and can perhaps drop a loop of line from a stern bridle or drop a spring line over the cleat and then click her into gear ahead to bring her in. The fact is that once the stern line is ashore the tide will very likely bring the boat alongside anyway. You will be hanging off the stern line or bridle.

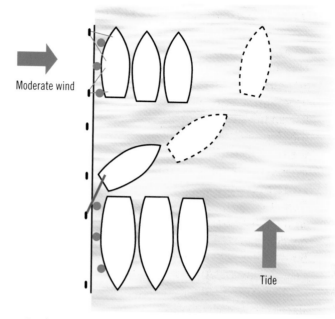

Moderate wind

Tide

▲ Berthing stern-to in a tricky berth between boats

▼ Here I have dropped a stern spring over the cleat and am demonstrating how, even if I get blown off the dock, I can still bring the boat alongside by driving against the spring

STRONG WIND BLOWING YOU OFF A STRETCH OF PONTOON

The stern approach
Given that the stern of all boats will find the wind when going backwards it should be possible to drive at 90° to the dock and drop or lasso a line over a cleat. Drive ahead against this and bring the boat alongside. You should be able to manage this single-handed.

The bows approach
Now drive the bow at 90° to the dock. This manoeuvre will require crew on the bow to drop the line over the cleat. (If there is a fair degree of shear to your bow you can probably have the crew leaning right over the shore cleat; if you have a modern plumb bow you can't.) Drive astern against this line to bring you alongside.

The MCA's position on motoring against springs

i

I am mindful that I should be advising 'safe practice' and so I contacted the Maritime Coastguard Agency (MCA) in January 2014 to ask them if they had a view on motoring against springs, or if they had ever made any ruling about this and this is what they told me:

> The MCA's surveyors are seafarers who apply their maritime knowledge to identify potential problems before they happen. They have never ruled that powering against a spring was unsafe and illegal. Indeed, they recognise the process of using a vessel's engine in combination with a suitably positioned spring is an appropriate way of berthing a vessel; however, there is a difference between berthing a vessel and boarding passengers. The MCA has stopped vessels powering against a single line while passengers are getting on and off to protect those who may not have any nautical knowledge or whose mobility may be impaired.

And they hold this view because they are the accountable authority.

It is always worth trying these techniques out in benign conditions on a nice stretch of pontoon with plenty of fairway room and no traffic, just to see what happens.

Remember that you are not using any of these techniques to stop the boat. The boat should be stationary, or very nearly so, when you attach yourself to the dock. You arrive, get the bridle line or spring ashore, drive against this until you are alongside, then you step ashore, moor the boat properly and take the engine out of gear.

BOX MOORING

Those who have box moorings will set their favoured arrangement of lines so they can be picked up as they enter the berth. They will pick up the windward set first. Some people lie along the posts first, get ahold of the lines and then warp the boat into the mooring. Others use their engine and a spring and back the boat in against this.

The system used will depend on the control you have when driving astern. Short-handed is best for box mooring. Although I believe that you could single-hand the boat in with a bridle. If you can drive up to the box, turn and present your quarter to the windward post, you can drop the bridle over the post and then go astern into the box.

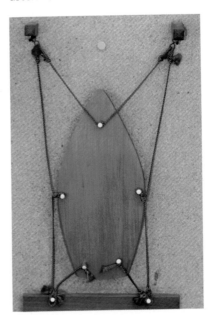

Mooring arrangement in a box mooring

⌘ Lie along the posts first.

⌘ Then pick up the lines and warp the boat in.

⌘ Alternatively, get a spring on.

⌘ Then back the boat in against it.

If your prop walk could be taking you up to windward at the same time this would be a bonus. If it does not, hook the windward spring line as soon as possible to keep going straight into the box. The bow cannot blow off as it is held to the windward post with the bridle. With the boat in the box, attach the windward stern line, then the windward bowline, release the bridle and set the leeward lines.

For the single-handed bridle technique it would be important to protect the boat from the post. It is easier to attach the protection to the post as the single-hander cannot hold a fender strategically in place throughout the manoeuvre. Thick carpet might be enough, although I would consider something more substantial like a dock fender. If stern-to single-handed isn't going to work, come in bows-to, pick up the windward spring line first, attach this amidships and then pick up the windward bow and stern lines.

TOP TIP

A simple creak preventer

Old mooring warps tend to creak as they come under tension and this can be very irritating, especially at night. Once the warps start doing this it's time to renew them. However, any rope can make a dreadful creaking sound if it is rubbing against a toe rail, but if you put a plastic bag between the rope and the toe rail the creaking disappears. It looks a bit weird, but it works.

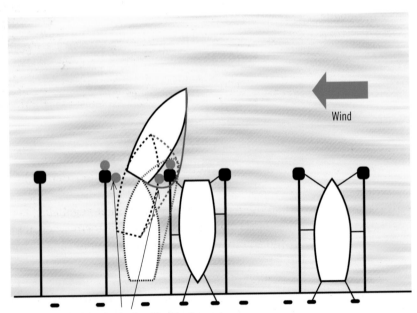

Use thick carpet or fenders (dock fender, pontoon fender or bumper dock) to protect the gunwhale

Box mooring single-handedly with a bridle

RAFTING UP

The key to rafting up is getting a centre line from you to the host boat as soon as you are alongside. This short line will keep you attached to the host boat and prevent you being pushed back with the tide or wind. You will have arrived alongside motoring into the tide, fenders set at gunwhale height. The host boat may well also have their fenders set at gunwhale height in anticipation of someone rafting up alongside.

The correct procedure as you draw close to them is to hail them by boat name and ask permission to raft up alongside. If there is no one on board, just carry on.

Bring the boat to a stop. You will have said to the harbour master or marina office that you kick to port when in astern and with any luck they will have given you a 'port to' raft-up. A few revs astern will tuck you in nicely. Attach the short midship line first. Now that you are secure you can hand over your lines. It can be a frightful faff to lead lines from you over to them, through their fairlead, around their cleat, back through their fairlead and back to you. Invariably when you might want to run slipped lines their crew will think that you want your lines OXO'd on their cleats. So it is much simpler to hand them a loop (just a bowline in the end of the line) and ask them to put this over their cleat. They can sort out running the line through their fairleads and so forth. Now you have control: adjust your bow line, stern line and springs as you like. And, of course, set shore lines so that you are not asking the host boat to take all your weight.

This short line amidships is key to rafting up

A bowline loop to the host boat works well

Leaving from the middle of a raft

The first question you need to ask a host boat after having requested permission to raft up alongside is what time they are leaving. It can be a little alarming to hear: 'We need to leave at 4 o'clock in the morning.' You always can try negotiating a little.

Occasionally there will be someone in the middle of the raft who would like to leave before those outside them. This is great because everyone comes together as a team to do this so there is very little tutting and generally everyone is good-humoured about it.

One option is for outside boats to un-raft themselves, stooge about until the leaving boat has gone

and then raft up again. That's what they did when I was inside two others in St Helier. I needed to time my run up the Alderney race (which is not negotiable) and other boats understood well. I told them when they arrived and they were happy to raft up then and let me out later.

Another option is to open out a raft. You need to prepare for this. Always open out a raft down tide, never with the tide. You don't want the tide splitting the raft apart. That could end in disaster. If you are down tide, the tide will be pushing the raft back together, which will help once the inside boat has gone.

LEAVING THE MIDDLE OF A RAFT OF THREE BOATS

■ The bow lines, stern lines, springs and shore lines for all three boats at the start. Photo: © Rod Lewis

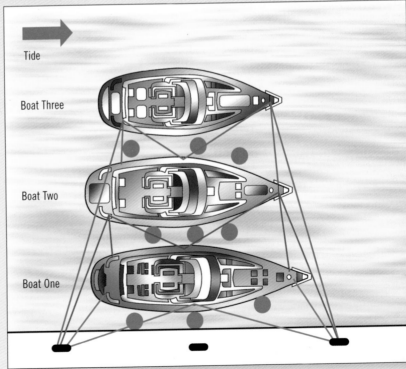

Tide

Boat Three

Boat Two

Boat One

■ Boat Two loses shore lines, then Boat Three adjusts shore lines so that the down tide shore line goes behind the departing Boat Two and up past the bow of Boat One to the shore. Boat Three sets a slipped stern line to Boat Two and loses her bow line and springs.

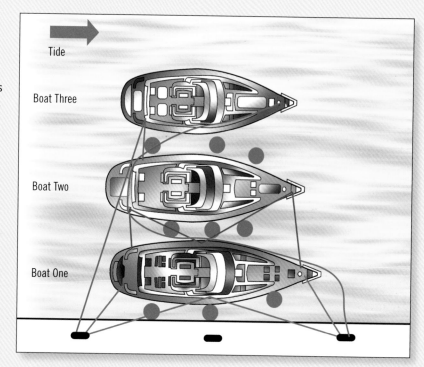

■ Boat Two sets a stern spring to Boat One to spring out the bow and puts her engine astern with enough revs to hold her and Boat Three against the tide (but not so many revs that she starts to open out the raft) and Boat Two loses her bow line, stern line and springs to Boat One – ready to go. Boat Two increases revs and starts to spring out her bow and break the raft apart. With the raft open enough Boat Two goes into neutral and retrieves the slipped spring. At the same time Boat Three releases the slipped stern line from them to Boat Two and then with a tickle of ahead Boat Two drives out of the raft.

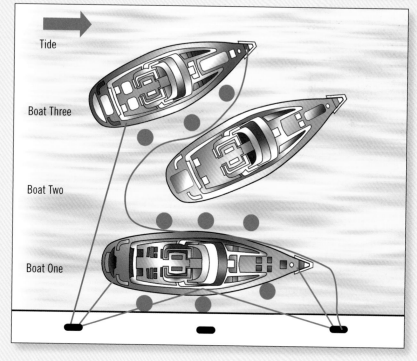

■ As soon as Boat Three is close enough to Boat One they hand over a stern line and then the bow line and springs. As Boat Three comes in she may need to click in a little astern to hold her against the tide. And that's it.

MEDITERRANEAN MOORING

End-on mooring is the order of the day in the Mediterranean – wonderful to be moored up right next to your table at the restaurant. You do see the occasional boat moored side on, but they run the risk of others rafting up on them. Sometimes the harbour will have lazy lines set, sometimes you will use your anchor.

One thing to be aware with Mediterranean mooring is that because many of the harbours have been built up with rocks and blocks of concrete tumbled on top of each other, the harbour walls that may look sheer above the water can be anything but below. Before coming in stern-to make sure that you won't be smacking your rudder into the rocks just under the surface. A quick look to see what everyone else is doing is the best plan.

Bows-to may be best. You can also find half finished and fairly rough quays with rusty reinforcing metal work sticking out, ready to damage our topsides. So we need to make sure that our anchor, be it bower or kedge, is holding us off the quay. In fact at night it is advisable in some places to ease the shore lines and wind in a good few metres of anchor cable so that we are held several metres off. Now when the high speed ferries go past their wash will not bounce us off the harbour wall.

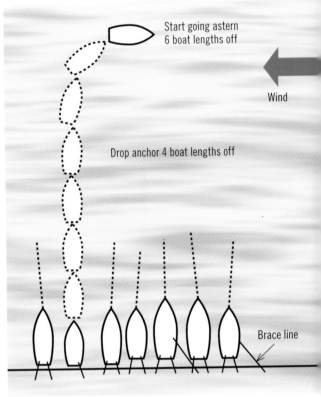

Start going astern 6 boat lengths off

Wind

Drop anchor 4 boat lengths off

Brace line

▲ *Mediterranean mooring stern-to using an anchor*

TOP TIP

Frap that halyard. It stops noise and saves on wear and chafe.

Mediterranean mooring, right next to the restaurant

Stern-to using an anchor

Line yourself up about six boat lengths away from your slot to counter any effect of prop walk when going astern and to get her driving straight before dropping the anchor. Then drop the hook four boat lengths away from the quay.

Keep driving gently astern until you are close to the quay and then stop the boat by giving a short burst of ahead and then putting her into neutral. Now it is a question of stepping ashore to attach the lines or handing them to someone on the shore to attach for you, securing the windward line first. Then we will nip up the anchor to tension the stern lines.

⌘ Mediterranean mooring approach.

⌘ Hand the lines ashore, windward line first.

⌘ A bollard ashore can be lassoed from on board.

⌘ To attach to chains, you will probably need to step off.

Bows-to using an anchor

Again, line yourself up with your slot and drop the kedge anchor four boat lengths away. Motor in gently, stop the boat and get the bow lines ashore, again securing the windward one first. Some boats have a plate welded to the bow roller so you can walk off the bow.

When bows-to, people often set up a gangplank. I set it when I need it and remove it when I don't to discourage rats. Harbours with piles of rubbish and un-emptied bins will have rats. Harbours that are smart and clean will probably also have rats but fewer.

Mediterranean mooring using an anchor is best done two-handed. I talked to seasoned Mediterranean sailors and asked them about single-handed mooring and they all said they wouldn't do it. Much better to have one other member of crew was the message.

That said, it is possible to moor stern-to single-handed if you have a windlass remote that can be operated from the cockpit. Position the boat, start to drive astern towards the slot, drop the anchor using the cockpit remote, arrive at the quay and stop the boat. Then attach the windward line. You may be faced with a number of attachment options ranging from bollards to rings or chains. It is important to fender up the stern

because whatever you are doing the boat will be close enough to the quay to be touching.

I am a great believer in self-sufficiency and not relying on others, but the Mediterranean is one place where (unless it is the middle of winter) there will always be someone ashore to take your lines, the restaurant owner probably, and that is a tremendous help.

Departing presents a problem for the single-hander because you need to be in two places at once – at the stern to handle the lines and at the bow to handle the anchor. You could do it with help from the shore and someone to let the stern lines go while you weigh anchor at the bow. With two people and the shore lines set to slip, you release them from on board and give the crew on the anchor controls at the bow the go-ahead to start bringing in the anchor. You always want to have someone at the bow when weighing anchor to make sure that the cable is coming in neatly, that you are not straining the windlass, that the cable is not piling up in the locker causing a jam and to see that the anchor is free to come up and not lying under someone else's.

When bringing the anchor up on a windlass slow it down or stop it as the anchor breaks the water and

Here they have taken the anchor off the bow roller to provide a step

Having a custom-made bucket for the kedge anchor and cable, welded to the pushpit, is a great idea for Mediterranean-based boats

Check that the anchor is free to come up and not lying under someone else's

before it feeds on to the bow roller to check that it is the right way up and to prevent it from swinging wildly as it comes on board. If the anchor needs cleaning then leaving it just under the surface, motoring ahead gently, should help. Motoring too fast will have the anchor gouging the gelcoat on the bow. You need to be cautious.

Arriving bows-to, single-handing is more difficult. It really is not possible to lay out the kedge anchor while helming the boat. The warp is easy enough, you can simply throw that over the stern, but the first 10 metres of the anchor cable should be chain and you're likely to damage the gel coat on the stern if you chuck out the anchor and then a bunch of chain.

Preparation

⌘ Fender up well. When mooring to anything that could damage the boat, add in a fender between the boat and the impending accident. Volcanic rock is wickedly sharp.

⌘ Whether stern-to or bows-to your lines should be readied and OXO'd on to the cleats. If you are not sure of the means of attaching the shore lines (rings, cleats, chain), keep the ends free so that the line can be returned to the boat for adjustment. If the quay has bollards you can a) tie a bowline in the end of the line and drop the loop over, b) bring the tugboat bowline into play for an instant loop (see Chapter 2) or c) lasso them.

⌘ Figure out the best way for you to helm backwards. It is often taught that the best way to helm backwards is to face backwards. In a boat with a wheel, this means standing the other side of the binnacle. This is all well and good except for the fact that the Morse control for the engine is now the wrong way round. We are going backwards and standing behind the binnacle the gear lever in astern is pointing 'forwards'. In a panic and approaching the quay a little too quickly I have seen the helm, on a number of occasions, push the gear lever 'forward' to stop the boat's backward progress to the quay. This 'forward' is, of course, astern and the boat has now rammed into the quay with a sickening thud. Many people are very comfortable with facing astern while driving astern, but I prefer facing more or less sideways so I can keep an eye on both our progress astern and on what the bow is doing. This is probably the result of having a boat whose handling astern is not the easiest.

⌘ Agree some simple signals between helm and crew (although clearly shouted instruction works for me). And just as important as a clearly shouted instruction is a clearly shouted confirmation that the instruction has been understood. 'Let go the anchor' from the helm should be followed by 'Anchor going down' from the crew to keep everyone in the picture.

Crosswinds

If there is a crosswind, you need to drop the anchor upwind of the slot you are aiming for. Don't worry too much about laying your anchor cable across another. This happens. The water is usually clear enough to see what is going where and arrange departures so that those with cables on top go first.

Now you need to steer your boat astern into the slot, fendered well on both sides but especially to leeward. The first line to go ashore will be the windward line. You may also set a brace from amidships to the shore. It is worth noting that the wind that has picked up in the late afternoon invariably dies down with sunset so a moderate crosswind at 4pm might have reduced to just enough to stir the flags a few hours later. It doesn't always go according to plan, of course.

⌘ Here, despite being attached to the shore, the breeze is blowing the bow into the bow next door.

⌘ Nipping up the anchor would sort this out and then adding in a brace line.

Lazy lines

These are lines that are laid from the quay to a sinker out in the harbour. Sometimes they are laid in pairs and sometimes singly. Drive astern into the slot, secure lines to the shore, then pick up the lazy line(s) and lead them to the bow, tension and secure and that's it. You can also arrive bows-in and secure the lazy line(s) to your stern. Mooring to a lazy line is much easier single-handed than using an anchor, because you don't have the anchor to worry about when coming into the slot.

Departing with lazy lines, it is important to drop the lazy lines first before driving off. Stern-to, set the stern lines to slip and drop the leeward line. Then drop the lazy line(s) and give them a moment to drop to the seabed out of the way of your stern gear and propeller before slipping the windward stern line and driving off. Bows-to the same applies.

Lead the lazy lines to the bow, tension and secure. INSET: A lazy line

When dropping the lazy line(s), give them a moment to drop to the seabed out of the way of your stern gear

FRENCH FINGERS AND HOOPED CLEATS

French finger berths are very much shorter, not to mention narrower, than anything we are accustomed to in the UK. Added to which some of them come with hooped cleats rather than T-shaped cleats so they are impossible to lasso. One way round this is to set a stern bridle and lasso the entire end of the finger.

If the finger is short and you're aproaching bows-in set the bridle as far forward as you can. However, if the finger berth has a bar at the end (and most do) and there is another boat on the other side of the finger then it is impossible to lasso the entire finger.

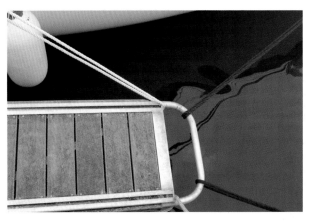

Mooring lines from the other boat make it impossible for us to lasso the entire finger

Lassoing the end of a French finger berth

I spent some time working on this problem. I called up Chantereyne Marina in Cherbourg, gave my French an airing and explained what I wanted. By which I mean I was passed fairly swiftly on to the very helpful and English-speaking Caroline who told me in answer to my questions that they had the full range of finger berths. So off we went. Three days in Cherbourg lassoing everything in site and we had the short, thin and wobbly French finger berths cracked – as long as there was no boat attached to the other side. Pretty much all of the fingers come with a bar at the end and so I decided that if I could get something down inside that bar with a line that ran to our midship cleat, I could drive against this. We scoured the harbour for short metal or stout plastic pipes that we could drop down between the bar and then which would lock against it when we pulled on it. Nothing we found was quite right – the risk of the pipe or bar slipping out was too great. Then we went to the chandlers and my eyes fell upon a toy grapnel anchor. That might do it. It cost €9 and worked beautifully. Drive the boat up to the finger, step out of the cockpit, lower the tiny anchor into the gap between bar and finger, haul in the line and click the engine into ahead. I needed to hold the collar out of the way. If that drops down then the grapnel will not fold up to go through the gap between bar and finger, which could be disappointing. Once through though, it splays out and holds you firmly.

If your boat is short enough a midship line to the T-cleat on the finger works fine. For my boat this would put the bow six feet through the end of the pontoon so I didn't try this, but driving against the end of the berth might work. Many people had hefty fenders to protect their bows.

Entering any unfamiliar port it is necessary either to call up and ask what cleats and berths they have or to putter down the line of fingers and investigate. Making sure you can execute a 180° turn in your own length or being able to motor astern comfortably is important.

 Scan this QR code to watch a video on these two techniques in action.

A well-fendered bow

If you don't speak French or your school French is rusty bone up on some useful vocabulary in advance. Hooped cleats are *taquets d'amarrage cercle*, T cleats *taquets d'amarrage en forme de T*. It's also a good idea to learn the weather terms to understand the French forecasts. Most French people will help you out if you try to speak French to them, or will find someone who can help.

Mooring devices

I prefer to use a line and lasso something ashore rather than use mooring devices. I do have a Moorfast and although I have never used it I am sure it would thread a line through a standard cleat or on to a French hooped cleat as quick as can be, as long as you did not hold the Moorfast too vertically above the cleat. The Hook and Moor looks like a handy piece of kit, too, although the rather narrow jaws and fairly chunky head mean it is limited in the gauge of ring or cleat it will fit round; on occasion it is too large to fit through or around some of the rings attached to mooring buoys. And then there are hooks with caribiner style gates which fit on to the end of the boat hook. I have seen these used for mooring and they seemed to be very effective.

⌘ Note the collar is held out of the way by some yellow tape.

⌘ Once through the grapnel splays out and holds you firmly.

⌘ Hooked on to the bar!

SAILING, HEAVING TO & REEFING

Setting the sails and trimming them so they perform as efficiently as possible is a matter of pride for me and by getting it right I go faster and the motion of the boat is more comfortable. Having the correct amount of sail set for the conditions is an important part of stress-free sailing. It really is not necessary to go screaming around at a heel of 45°. In fact, it is to be avoided. All boats will heel to some degree, but too much heel simply spills wind from the top of the sails and you are much better off reducing sail and sailing more upright.

Raising the main while under headsail

SAIL TRIM AND HANDLING

There are many excellent books on sail trim worth consulting. As a general rule, if the tell tales on the headsail are flying straight, the only noise we can hear is the rush of water past the hull and your boat speed seems reasonable, all is well.

A flappy sail is not a happy sail. It may sound corny, but it's true. Eric Hiscock talked about putting 'his sails to sleep'. When they were asleep he knew they were trimmed to perfection. A flapping or a fluttering noise is the sail telling us that it's not as efficient as it could be and asking to be trimmed.

Raising the main

Remember you are not just lifting a sail on a halyard when you raise the main, you are also hoisting a whole lot of cordage, the reefing lines, and are faced with a huge amount of friction (the resistance of sliders in the mast track, turning blocks and lines to the cockpit running through jamming blocks etc). To help reduce this, pull out the reefing lines at the end of the boom so that they don't have to run the gamut of obstructions. It makes a fair mess in the cockpit, but it makes raising the main easier.

People generally raise the main while under engine by turning the boat head to wind. I prefer to do this while under headsail. To do this, sail close-hauled (see page 92) and ease the main sheet so the boom is lying directly downwind.

The advantages of doing this are:

- No slatting of the boom. Being on a point of sail you will have a little heel and the boom will lean off to leeward. And with no slatting you are less likely to break anything or suffer from chafe. Or get clouted by the boom.

▲ Close-hauled, car back, trimmed nicely ▼ Downwind, car forward, trimmed nicely. Both photos: © Rick Buettner

⌘ I have started using a very lazy technique to hoist the main: I use my electric windlass.

⌘ Being a horizontal windlass this works. Certain vertical windlasses will also work, but those that are housed in foredeck lockers will not, as the main halyard needs to run from the winch at the mast to the windlass and the angle it makes with certain windlasses means that it will slip off.

- The boat is more stable.
- If you're on starboard tack you're in the ascendancy over port tackers and those under engine (I said 'in the ascendancy' because there is no right of way in the collision regulations).
- You save money by using less diesel.

There are some boats for which raising the main under headsail is not possible because the boom needs to be in line with the mast, otherwise the sliders and batten cars can jam in the main track. *Southern Cross*, a Rustler 36, mentioned this being a problem.

Fully battened sails and lazy jacks

If you just have lazy jacks on their own keeping them out of the way when raising the main and setting them when handing it is the order of the day. You can't do this with a stack pack as lazy jacks have to be set the whole time and these invariably catch a top batten as the sail is raised. Loosening the lazy jacks makes things worse and so tight lazy jacks with stack packs is generally best. One thing I notice with lazy jacks

TOP TIP

Jib halyards and sheets are usually blue, spinnaker halyards and sheets red, but here's some neat colour coding on an in-mast furling system. Green for 'go' for the outhaul and red for 'stop' for the furler.

and stack packs is that the lazy jacks are often set very high and very close in. If you can lower them the chances of catching a batten as you raise the sail are reduced significantly. The same applies if you can take them further apart, say, along the spreader. Partially battened or battenless sails don't suffer from this, of course.

In-mast furling mainsails

In-mast furling mainsails are a great invention for general sailing, although some people still treat them with suspicion: 'the potential for jamming', 'all that weight up the mast when furled', etc. Apparently, we have the flotilla sailors in the Med to thank for in-mast furling as it was developed to make life easy for them. When pulling out the sail it is best to be slightly on the wind, rather than directly head-to. This allows the wind to draw the sail out. When furling in, being on the wind keeps a little pressure in the sail for a nice tight wrap. A beam reach on port with the boom eased out worked well when we tested this on a Beneteau Oceanis 393.

Unfurling the headsail

When hauling in on the sheet and allowing a furling headsail to unfurl, keep a little tension on the furling line. Occasionally if there is no tension and the sail unfurls in a hurry you can end up with a riding turn on the furler as the furling line reels in quickly. This presents a problem as you cannot either furl or unfurl the headsail using the furling line and you will need to unwrap the headsail around the forestay until it is fully out and you can then bring it down off the foil (unless you are able to take the drum apart and sort out the riding turn). Not easy. So part of the preparation for setting the headsail is to take the sheet round one winch and the furling line round another to be able to control the speed at which it unfurls.

SNAG-FREE SHEETS

■ When I tie the jib sheets to the clew with bowlines I tie them in such a way that the smooth side of the bowline of each sheet faces the shrouds and stays so there is less to snag.

■ You can also use one long line for the sheets and attach it to the clew with a cow hitch. It doesn't slip and there's even less to snag on shrouds and stays.

Wire–rope combinations sometimes only have enough room on the drum for the wire and perhaps a couple of turns of the rope. I change headsails from No 1 genoa to No 2 quite regularly and I need to make sure I have set the furling line correctly each time. I adjust it so the furling line goes from rope to wire just before it arrives at the drum when the sail is unfurled. It's worth checking the system to make sure that the sail will unfurl and furl with ease.

▼ *When attaching a headsail to the foil and furling system make sure that there is enough room on the drum to take all the rope or wire and rope combination when the sail is unfurled*

Sailing nearly 30° by the lee

Cruising chute by the lee: speed 5.5 knots in what looks like 14 knots of true wind. Who says you can't run downwind with a cruising chute

Downwind under cruising chute alone

I often set the cruising chute. When used in conjunction with the main, you can manage apparent wind angles of anywhere from as little as 70° to as much as 150°. However, to run dead downwind with the cruising chute, I hand the main. Now without a main the cruising chute can sail quite happily by the lee.

It's worth checking out what what wind angles your cruising chute will handle. Running downwind with a sail that isn't going to gybe the minute the wind gets behind it is a great comfort.

TOP TIP

Keep an eye on your apparent wind speed when sailing downwind. It's easy to be lulled into a false sense of security. Sailing downwind at 6 knots with 20 knots (force 5) of apparent wind speed means the true wind speed is actually about 25 knots (force 6). If you now turn round and beat back into this and maintain 6 knots of boat speed your apparent wind speed increases to something like 32 knots and that is force 7 – lots of wind.

⌘ Mainsheet twist.

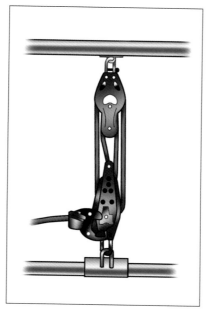

⌘ Using fiddle blocks.

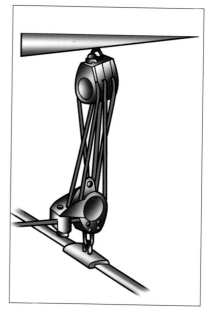

⌘ Right-angle reeving.

Mainsheet twist

What can you do about mainsheet twist? You set off with your mainsheet falls perfectly ordered and by the time you've crossed the bay they have twisted. Hauling in a mainsheet with twisted blocks and the falls dangling all over the place is a drag. What can you do?

If your boat is under 28 feet or so and using a four-part tackle you can use fiddle blocks to sort out mainsheet twist. Fiddle blocks tend not to twist. Even one fiddle block used with a standard block will help to reduce twist. With six-part tackles you don't have this option, but you can unreeve the sheet, remove the twist and re-reeve it. I have heard that trailing the sheet astern while under engine is one way to remove the twist, being careful not to let it get near the propeller, of course. Or you can reeve the blocks at 90° to each other to reduce twist.

Preventers

If the wind is flukey or you're concerned about gybing accidentally while sailing downwind rigging a preventer is a good idea. I set this from the end of the boom to a bow cleat, run the line back to the cockpit and on to a winch and harden up. To save yourself the faff of having to reset it when you gybe, set up two preventers, one either side. Slacken off the active preventer before gybing and harden up the new preventer when through the gybe.

Jib or genoa? ?

A jib is a headsail whose foot does not reach past the mast. A genoa is a headsail whose foot reaches past the mast.

SAILING IN A CIRCLE ON THE SPOT

There are two key things we need to practise: sailing in a circle on the spot and heaving to. Often our time out on the water is so precious that instead of practising and experimenting we set sail for a destination and that's it. But if we can just take a moment to play, I think we learn a lot. And the more we play the more control we have over the boat and this will be handy in an emergency.

One of the first things I do on any boat is to sail her in a circle on the spot. I will centre the main and then tack her without touching the sheets. With the helm down to leeward she will immediately go into the heave-to position. By keeping the helm down, I will keep her going around in a circle. She may hang slightly before gybing. Some heavy boats may be difficult to gybe round if the wind is light.

I want to find out how quickly I can spin her round, what control I have, how well she will sail to windward with the headsail backed. This will be the key to getting back to our man overboard under sail. It is definitely worth practising sailing in a circle without touching anything just to see how a boat behaves. Can you stop her at any point by turning to windward? And how quickly does the bow blow off?

HEAVING TO

Then I will see how a boat heaves to. This is a most useful technique: if you can stop your boat in the water then you can have a rest. You will also heave to as part of your heavy weather strategy – see Chapter 9.

You heave to by tacking without touching the headsail sheets so that when you come on to the new tack the headsail is aback – just like you did when you sailed around in a circle. Only this time you will put the helm about 20–25 degrees down to leeward on the new tack. This is to help the mainsail drive the bow to windward against the opposing force of the wind on the backed headsail pushing the bow to leeward. The result should be little or no boat speed.

Boats with a deep fore-foot will heave to comfortably without fore-reaching and have little or no boat speed when hove to. Modern boats with little draught forward are more difficult to bring to a stop and can tack themselves out of the heave-to position.

■ Hove to.

By playing with the variables you can get modern fin-keel boats to heave to quietly. It is all a question of adjusting the balance. The variables to adjust are:

- Sail size
- Sail balance
- Sail trim
- Helm adjustment
- Centre board adjustment

Ideally you want your log to read 0 knots. Although if you're stopping for a rest or for lunch, it does not matter if you're fore-reaching slowly at 1–1.5 knots. Be aware of 'sea room' though. If there is a 1.5 knot tide running, not only will you be making way forward at, say, 1–1.5 knots you will also be drifted down tide 1.5 miles every hour. Add in another 0.5 knot for leeway. So you will need sea room ahead of up to 1.5 miles and down tide of 2 miles before you might hit anything, in order to have a lunch hour in peace.

In any kind of sea, it is amazing to see how the motion of the boat changes when you heave to. Where you were bouncing along, now hove-to the

■ Gybing out of the hove-to position.

■ On the other tack.

motion is much calmer. You need to practise heaving to in different wind strengths. Hove-to you should lie between 40° and 50° to the wind.

In terms of sail balance and how much sail you require, as the wind strengthens you'll find that there is sufficient windage on the bow to be able to hand the headsail and lie hove-to under reefed main alone. If you have a furled headsail, this provides extra windage on the forestay to help push the bow to leeward. I find that in 25 knots of wind I can heave to with just a reefed main.

It is dangerous to generalise which is why you need to practise with your own boat, but ketches can heave to in very strong winds with just a reefed mizzen, schooners can set a reefed main and a backed foresail or staysail.

Finally on heaving to, it is a very good idea to heave to on starbord, because that way most other vessels will have to give way to you. And this means that it's a good idea if your galley is to port as it is marginally easier cooking with a slight downhill tilt than a slight uphill tilt. Mine is to starboard – I wonder why Hallberg-Rassy didn't think that one through?

Scan this QR code to watch a video on sailing in a circle on the spot.

Scan this QR code to watch a video on heaving to.

TOP TIP

Mark the centre of the helm on the wheel. A Turks's head knot or a piece of tape will do. There are helm position indicators, but they are not always easy to see. With a mark on the wheel, you can feel when the helm is centred without having to lose your concentration.

REEFING

Very few people speak well of single-line jiffy reefing systems. You're supposed to be able to do everything from the cockpit. However, the strain put on that one line to bring down the tack and the clew with all the friction associated with more than six changes in direction of pull on that line mean that a snarl-up soon occurs. To sort this, you have to go to the mast, which defeats the object of 'one line led to the cockpit'. For operation from the cockpit, double-line reefing works fine. Slab reefing where you attach the cringle to the ram's horn at the mast is also an excellent system.

Reefing drill

This is my routine with a slab-reefed main and mast winches:

1. Kicker off.
2. Topping lift on.
3. Set lazy jacks.
4. Sail close-hauled.
5. Ease mainsheet so the boom is lying dead downwind.
6. Ease halyard.
7. Put cringle on ram's horn.
8. Harden up main halyard.
9. Harden up reefing line.
10. Topping lift off.
11. Kicker on.
12. Sheet in main.
13. Tie in reefing ties to hold bunt.

Reefing the main on a beam or broad reach?

I can't do this on my boat. With a fully battened main, I need to line the boom up with the wind. The same goes for friends of mine with partially battened mainsails. According to Lin Pardey, with a batten-less main you can reef on any point of sail. I have also heard of those with fully battened mains and very powerful winches on the boom and at the mast being able to reef when sailing downwind. The strain from the compression on the batten cars and the sliders must be considerable. So some can and some can't. It depends on your set-up and the style of your mainsail.

Reefing from the cockpit

Slab reefing tips
Getting the cringle on the ram's horn

Slab reefing means you have to ease the halyard, pull down the sail and get the cringle on the ram's horn, then harden up. But the cringle often slips off before you can haul on the halyard. Use a reefing tie to hold the cringle on the ram's horn.

⌘ The cringle often slips off the ram's horn.

⌘ No more slipping off.

Loose footed main?

Tie the bunt on top of the boom and not round the boom. Tying it round the boom could result in the main blowing out in very strong wind. The reefing ties through the reefing points create a perforated, tear-off effect, especially if the sail is old and the fabric perhaps a little weak.

Reefing ties

Tying the reefing ties in with a slip knot so that they come out with one pull is important.

Tie the bunt on top of the boom

QUICK-RELEASE REEFING TIES

■ Take the running end of the tie through the eyelet and then through the eye splice.

■ Take the running end under the standing part to form a bight.

■ Now pull a bight of the running end through the first bight.

■ Pull tight. The reefing tie won't slip and yet you can free it with one tug.

Stack packs

When it comes to stack packs they say that when reefed you just let the bunt of the sail lie in the pack without having to secure it with reefing ties. I am sure this is fine for certain conditions but I wouldn't want to try this with three reefs in the main and 40+ knots of wind.

The bunt just sits in the stack pack

MOORING BUOYS

There are two general types of mooring buoy; those with a pendant and pick-up buoy and those with a simple iron hoop or ring at the top. We're going to pick up both of these single-handed.

APPROACH AND CONTROL OF THE BOAT

The first thing you need to do is to be able to control the boat. Whatever system you use for picking up the mooring, you will need to bring the boat up to the mooring buoy and hold it there for a moment. You'll want the pick-up float somewhere between amidships and the cockpit. If you're picking up a mooring buoy in the middle of a line of buoys and there is a boat moored ahead and one astern you need to be careful that by running past the mooring buoy so that it is amidships you're not running into the stern of the boat moored ahead.

Before you even attempt to get close to the mooring buoy position yourself nearby facing into the tide to get a measure of its strength. If the tide is weak you may find that ticking the engine ahead and then slowing so that you have very little forward motion and then putting it into neutral gives you a moment before the boat starts to fall back with the tide. If the tide is very strong (3–4 knots), you might find that you have to leave the engine in gear to hold the boat steady. Check this out before approaching the buoy, to make sure you can control the boat to give you that moment when she is stationary beside the buoy. It doesn't matter if you're single-handed or fully crewed, the helmsman must be able to judge this and position the boat perfectly.

How many times have you seen crew grab the pick-up buoy with the boathook and then have their arms wrenched out of their sockets as they try to hold the boathook while the helm over runs the buoy or allows the boat to slide back with the tide? Eventually they

Mooring buoy with a pendant and pick-up buoy

Mooring buoy with a ring at the top

Moored or anchored? **?**

- If you lie to one anchor, you are anchored.
- If you lie to two anchors you are moored.
- If you lie to a mooring buoy, you are moored.
- If you lie to a pile mooring, you are moored.

PREPARATION ROUTINE FOR PICKING UP A BUOY USING A BRIDLE

■ Take a turn around the port bow cleat.

■ Take the line forward of the stem head.

■ To prepare, take a spinnaker sheet, attach one end to a cockpit winch on one side (port in this example). Take this under the lower guard wire and outside the boat and up to the bow.

■ Up to the starboard cleat with a turn round this.

■ Bring the line outside everything back down the boat under the lower guard wire and up to a cockpit winch.

let go of the boathook and now not only are they not attached to the mooring they have also lost the boathook. So they have to go chasing after that before they can get back to the job of trying to moor.

And here's a point. The minute you get the boathook out to do anything it's a good idea to attach it to the boat, just in case (or you could carry a spare). In Chapter 2 I suggested a length of line attached at one end to the boathook and at the other to the boat with a rustler's hitch. Using rustler's hitches will allow us to free either end instantly and yet hold fast if the boathook does go in. Do I do this every time? No. Do I have to go chasing after the boathook because I've dropped it in the drink? Occasionally.

If you're short-handed the crew can show the helmsman where the buoy is by pointing to it the whole time with the boathook. If you're on your own you will lose sight of the buoy as it comes in under your bow, but it will come back into view as you bring it amidships.

When you approach the mooring buoy you need to be to leeward of it. You don't want to give your topsides a good work-out against the buoy by being blown on to it or, worse still, blown over it. If that happens there is the danger of bashing the buoy against your prop. Not ideal. I have seen a boat do just this. He was lucky and got away with it.

I have talked about approaching the mooring buoy under engine and you need to practise this until you are confident that whatever the conditions, however little room you have to manoeuvre, you can do it. You can also do this under sail, of course. Under main for wind forward of the beam and under headsail for wind abaft the beam.

The only difference between sail and engine is that with an engine de-powering is a matter of putting the gear lever into neutral and with sail it is a matter of getting the power of the wind out of the sail. And how you do this depends to some degree on the type of boat you have. I don't advocate picking up a buoy single-handed in a crowded mooring while under sail until you have practised and have it down to a fine art, because there is much to do and a lot of it at the same time.

Now that you have practised controlling the boat under engine, slowing down, stopping her or holding her steady for a moment against the given tide and wind strengths, you need to decide how you're going to pick up the buoy.

MOORING BUOY WITH PENDANT AND PICK-UP FLOAT

If there is very little tide and no wind to speak of, come alongside this buoy, get the boathook under the line of the pick-up float and lift it up. Get hold of the pendant, put the boathook down on the side deck. Walk the pendant to the bow and slip it over the bow cleat. However, if there is any tide running and a breeze, use a bridle to pick up this type of buoy.

Picking up the buoy using a bridle

You can do this in such a way that you also prepare for your single-handed departure. Again, everything is controlled from the cockpit.

After going through the preparation routine, you're now ready to pick the buoy up on either side. You will know in advance which side to pick it up because you will know the state of the tide and the wind direction. But setting the bridles up this way you have prepared 50% of your exit strategy, too. You want to have the buoy on your windward side so that you will be blown away from it. Having said that there are occasions in light winds where I have brought the buoy under my lee and used the wind to hold me on to it. Again, this is something that you learn with practice. Get the boathook ready. Lay it on the side deck if possible, clear of any line.

⌘ I have used this technique in quite blustery conditions.

⌘ You can always control the angle of the boat to the buoy and the wind by using the engine and the rudder.

HOW TO PICK UP A BUOY

■ Approach the buoy.

■ Slow to a stop alongside the buoy.

■ Pick up the line for the pick-up float with the boathook.

■ Pull it up and put the boathook down on the side deck.

■ Bring the pendant under the lower guard wire, take the bridle off the winch, thread it through the pendant.

■ Put the bridle back on the winch.

■ And wait.

■ You can get the pendant to the bow quicker if you click in a little astern to help the boat fall back with the tide.

■ Make your way up forward.

■ Slip the pendant on the cleat.

Slipping the mooring

The beauty of this set-up is that as the pendant has the bridle threaded through it, you are all set to slip the mooring. There are just two things to do:

- Take the line off the port winch and take it to the bow.
- Take the turn off the bow cleat, bring the line inside the shrouds back to the cockpit winch and secure. Do the same for the starboard side.

Now when you want to leave, take the pendant off the bow cleat (it has the line running through it) and when you let it go you will hang off this. You may not have enough time to release the pendant at the bow and walk back to the cockpit to drive off the mooring before you run back into the boat behind. So hanging off the slipped bridle allows you to control your exit from the cockpit.

Release one end of the bridle – the free end, the one without any snap shackle attached if you're using a spinnaker sheet as I am since that is my longest line – and haul in on the other end. You won't slip back much by doing this and if you did you could tick ahead on the

engine to maintain position. The key thing is that you are in the cockpit to do this and from there you can manage everything.

Addressing any concerns about the line in the water, there will be a short length of line that goes in the water, but this will be only the length of the distance from your bow to the mooring pendant, doubled. By leading the bridle inside the port bow cleat, out around the stem head and back inside the starboard bow cleat you make sure that very little line is able to dangle in the drink. You're hauling it in throughout this manoeuvre and the boat is going backwards so there is no chance of the line getting caught up in the prop or stern gear.

If you don't have a line long enough to go from a winch in the cockpit on one side round the bow and back to a winch in the cockpit on the other side, you can set the bridle for coming on to the buoy on one side only.

Departing when you don't have a single line that will run the distance you can use two lines joined together. You need to make sure that the join is inboard and this is the end you will haul on so that any line running through the pendant will be smooth.

Hanging off the pendant on the bridle. The lines of the bridle now lead inboard, along the deck inside the shrouds to the cockpit

The lines are now inside ready to slip

Two lines joined together. Make sure the join is on the inboard end

SLIPPING THE MOORING

■ Ready to release the port line and haul in on the starboard line.

■ Haul in until you're free.

■ Free and a short length of line in the water.

■ Where there is plenty of room you can drop back quite a bit.

PICKING UP A BUOY USING A SPINNAKER SHEET

■ Start by clipping the snap shackle to the guard rail by the cockpit.

■ Take the line outside everything to the bow and then lead it to the forward end of the bow cleat on the side on which you will be approaching the buoy and bring this line back along the side deck and inside the shrouds to the cockpit and secure on a winch. Leave some slack in this line.

■ Come up to the buoy and lift the line for the pick-up float out with the boathook.

■ Place the boathook down carefully and then, unclipping the snap shackle from the guard rail, thread this through the eye on the pendant and clip it back on the standing part of the spinnaker sheet.

■ Drop back against this as the tide pushes you back. At the same time, haul in the spinnaker sheet so that rather than hanging off a very long line you'll keep the buoy near the boat and very soon have the buoy by the bow.

Picking up the buoy using a spinnaker sheet

There is another way we can pick up a mooring buoy with a pendant and that is by using a spinnaker sheet or any long line with a snap shackle in one end.

MOORING BUOY WITH NO PENDANT

You are going to need to lasso this. There are a number of options for this:

Using the boathook and a large bight of rope (for very little tide only)

This is not really favoured by me as it is a rather flimsy affair and I like systems that do all the work for me. But if conditions are very benign (practically no tide, no wind), you can use this system. I would probably still use a bow bridle, one where I lassoed the buoy and allowed the boat to slip back and leave the buoy at the bow.

Approach to leeward of the buoy and drape the loop over the buoy. Use a line that will sink quickly, such as polyester three-strand or braid, Kevlar or Vectran. Nylon sinks slowly and polypropylene floats as does Dyneema. I will use three-strand polyester. Once the loop is over the buoy, put the boathook down carefully on the side deck, take the line to the bow and attach it with an OXO to a bow cleat and then prepare a more permanent mooring line, assuming that you will stay for a while.

Using a rope lasso (for little tide)

If the buoy has any sort of bow wave this may not be man enough for the job. Take a rope, wet it and join the ends. If the rope is joined you can't lose an end.

Again, approach to leeward of the buoy but not too close. If you lasso and the line hasn't sunk underneath the buoy, it may slip back over the top. If you lasso slightly to the side and the line hasn't gone under the mooring buoy then that extra lateral element should mean that it won't slip off.

So position your boat about 1 metre off the buoy. Remember to throw the lasso wide. With the buoy lassoed walk the end of the lasso to the bow and attach

The large loop is held in place and open by the boathook

I would definitely tape the line to the boathook as described in Chapter 2, because the line always falls off the boathook

to a cleat. The whole lasso being a loop you could just place it around a cleat as a temporary measure. Then attach yourself properly to the buoy.

Using a bridle (for moderate tide and wind)

In moderate tide and wind, you can also use a bridle. Simply lasso the buoy and then hang off the bridle. Set the bridle up by making one end fast at or near the bow. Run the line outside everything to the stern and secure on a winch. Have enough slack in the line to prepare four coils for the lasso. Approach the buoy into the tide and to leeward of it and lasso the buoy. Allow the tide to drop the boat back on the buoy or assist with engine astern. Attach a mooring line or two to the iron ring on the top of the buoy.

PICKING UP A BUOY USING A BRIDLE

■ Ready to lasso.

■ Lasso in action.

■ Allow the tide to drop the boat back on the lassoed buoy.

Using a heavy-duty lasso and bridle (for a strong tide)

If the buoy has its own bow wave or is awash you are going to need something beefy to go over and sink quickly. So you will make up a heavy-duty lasso. With one end made fast at the bow, the other on a winch in the cockpit, approach to leeward of the buoy and swing the heavy-duty lasso over it. It will sink. The boat will slide back and the buoy will arrive at the bow.

Mooring lines from boat to buoy

When there is no mooring pendant you need to supply your own mooring lines. If you're only staying for a short while a slipped line should be fine. The slipped line will chafe on the iron hoop or ring of the mooring buoy. If you're staying more than a couple of hours a proper mooring is required. Options are:

- a line from the boat to the buoy with a turn around the mooring buoy hoop or ring and then back to the boat

- a line from the boat and then a round turn and two half hitches (or an anchor bend) on the mooring buoy hoop or ring

The cautious among us will run two lines and this is certainly advisable if strong winds are forecast.

It may be that the buoy is some distance below you and you are unable to get down to it in the first instance. In that case, a mooring device might help to get a line through the hoop. Then with a line attached to the buoy you can generally lift the buoy up out of the water and fix your preferred system. I generally hoist up the buoy with the bridle line (which is caught round the chain of the buoy). If you can't get the buoy up and you are staying for a while you will need to get the dinghy out. Or the harbour master or whoever turns up to collect the mooring fee (because sure as eggs is eggs someone will turn up and ask for money) could be asked to assist. If you have set up a proper mooring and it is not possible to reach down to the buoy and its iron ring then you will need to get back into the dinghy to set the line to slip for departure.

Buoy with a bow wave

Heavy-duty lasso: polyester rope, 3/8ths chain in a plastic pipe

⌘ Dropping the heavy-duty lasso over the buoy.

⌘ The boat will slide back.

Slipping the mooring buoy

This is simple if there is little tide running or if there is no one near you. If there is quite a bit of tide and you don't have time to release at the bow and get back to the cockpit to drive ahead before you might run into the boat behind, then use the slipped bridle and hang off this. This works for both a pendant and a buoy with an iron ring or bar.

ANCHORING

Let's look at the essential considerations for choosing a spot to anchor first:

- **Shelter:** Check it's not a lee shore or likely to become one and that there are no nasty tides.
- **Not prohibited:** Make sure you're not in a fairway, shipping lane or restricted/prohibited area.
- **Depth:** What is it now? Is there enough depth at LW and do you have enough chain/warp for HW?
- **Holding:** Is there good holding for your type of anchor? (Generally, mud and sand are good, rock and shells not so good.)
- **Swinging room:** Is there enough room to swing when the tide turns?

Then we need ground tackle that is up to the job.

CODING THE CABLE

There is only one major stress-free tip that I have for anchoring and that is to calibrate the anchor cable. If you know how much cable you have veered you can sleep peacefully at anchor. When I can afford the superyacht I am sure there will be a digital readout in metres of the cable as it is paid out by the windlass. In the meantime, I need to mark the cable with something that I understand and that will not foul the chain on the gypsy. Many people put a splodge of red paint every 10 metres, but I cannot for the life of me remember when I have returned suitably refreshed from the pub how many splodges of paint I have let out. I'd recommend marking the chain in 5-metre intervals: This is more useful when you're anchoring in shallow water and I often anchor in 3 or 4 metres.

Anchoring gone wrong

How would they know how much chain they let out?

Fisherman's anchor

CQR or plough anchor

Bruce anchor

Fortress anchor

Rocna, one of the modern-type anchors

Grapnel

ANCHOR OPTIONS

Type	Make	For	Against	Bottom
Fisherman	Fisherman	Folds flat. Good on rock and kelp	Poor power to weight ration	Rock/kelp
Plough	CQR/plough	Good all rounder	Can trip when the tide turns but usually resets itself	All types, except rock and kelp
	Delta	Strong, sets quickly, self launching		All types, except rock and kelp
	Kobra	Strong, sets quickly, self launching		All types, except rock and kelp
Claw	Bruce	Strong	No moving parts, has to be mounted on the bow roller	All type, except rock and kelp
Modern	Spade	Strong, sets quickly, self launching	Breaks down into sections so can stow flat	All types, except rock and kelp
	Rocna	Strong, sets very quickly, self launching	Check the quality of the steel, some were made with inferior steel	All types, except rock and kelp
	Manson Supreme	Strong, sets very quickly, clever self tripping slot		All types, except rock and kelp
Flat	Danforth	Folds flat	Shingle can jam it	Sand
	Fortress	Folds flat	Shingle can jam it	Sand
	Brittany	Folds flat	Shingle can jam it	Sand
Grapnel	Grapnel	Folds up	Used as a kedge anchor or for dinghies	Anything except rock and kelp

Snooker

For some reason I seem to be able to remember the order in which to pot snooker balls, despite not playing the game. And so I mark my chain with silks tied in at 5-metre intervals in this order. And because that only gets me to 35 metres and my chain is 50 metres I go back to the beginning and double up:

- 1 x Red   =   5m
- 1 x Yellow =   10m
- 1 x Green   =   15m
- 1 x Brown   =   20m
- 1 x Blue   =   25m
- 1 x Pink   =   30m
- 1 x Black   =   35m
- 2 x Red   =   40m
- 2 x Yellow =   45m

Alphabetically

If snooker means nothing to you here's an alternative:

- 1 x Black   =   5m
- 1 x Blue   =   10m
- 1 x Brown   =   15m
- 1 x Green   =   20m
- 1 x Pink   =   25m
- 1 x Red   =   30m
- 1 x Yellow =   35m
- 2 x Black   =   40m
- 2 x Blue   =   45m

You can, of course, use any system you wish, but the ones I mention make sense.

 Scan this QR code to watch a video on coding the cable.

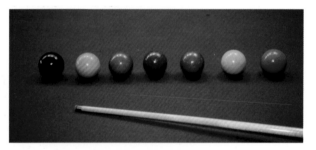

▲ The snooker code: red, yellow, green, brown, blue, pink, black

▲ Cable markers on warp

▼ Chain marked with silks tied at five-metre intervals in the snooker code

▼ If I see a piece of pink silk flying above the water I know I have 30m of cable out

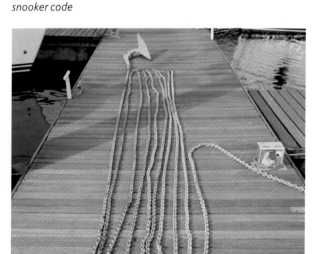

Do the silks last long? This is what they looked like after three years of anchoring and being kept in the filthy anchor locker along with the rusty chain

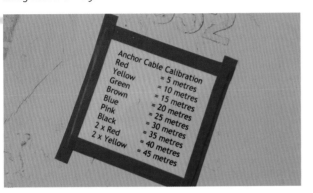

Anchor Cable Calibration
Red = 5 metres
Yellow = 10 metres
Green = 15 metres
Brown = 20 metres
Blue = 25 metres
Pink = 30 metres
Black = 35 metres
2 x Red = 40 metres
2 x Yellow = 45 metres

Put your code inside a foredeck locker lid so that new crew know what it all means

If the cable is mainly warp with only 10 metres of chain or so between the anchor and the warp, you can either tie the silks into the strands of the three-strand or multi-plait or bind coloured cotton around. Now with a system like this you know precisely how much cable is out.

Rust can weaken anchor chain. Surface rust can be brushed off, but you should check each link of the chain every so often. Also make sure that the shackle attaching the chain to the anchor is securely 'moused'; it is usual to use wire for this.

▼ *Here I have used a cable tie to mouse the shackle attaching the anchor to the chain. Cable ties degrade quite quickly and need to be checked regularly*

QUICK TIPS FOR ANCHORING SUCCESS

Setting the anchor

If there is very little tide running you may want to run the boat astern to make sure the anchor has dug in. I always find my 45lb CQR on 3/8th chain sets fine by just allowing the boat to settle back with the tide. In non-tidal waters backing up to set the anchor will help.

How much scope?

For peace of mind the rule is a minimum of four times depth for chain and a minimum of six times depth for warp.

When calculating depth don't forget to allow an extra metre for the distance from bow roller to water. And if the wind is likely to pipe up veer a little extra cable, assuming you have room in the anchorage.

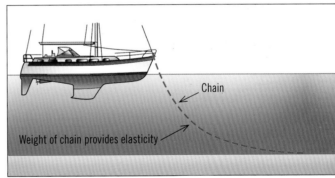

Chain

Weight of chain provides elasticity

Chain: catenary effect

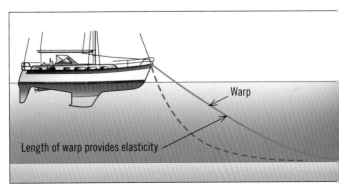

Warp

Length of warp provides elasticity

Warp: elasticity

Snubber at work

Check your bearings

Snubber

I always attach a piece of line to the chain using a rolling hitch, then make the line fast to a cleat and run the chain out until it goes slack and the tension is taken on the line. Apart from taking the pressure off my expensive windlass, this also acts as a snubber.

How to tell if your anchor is holding

The first way is to place your hand outside the bow roller on to the cable. If it is quiet, you are holding; if it is vibrating, you may be on the move. Fixing something on the shore and monitoring this by eye or bearing is another way and setting your anchor watch on the GPS is another.

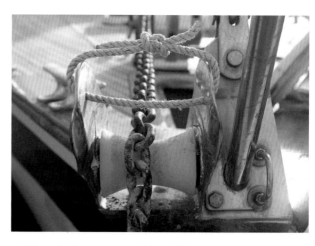

▲ *Using a lashing to prevent the cable from jumping off the bow roller*

▼ *Using a drop nose pin to prevent the cable from jumping off the bow roller*

Preventing the cable from jumping off the bow roller

A drop nose pin or a lashing across the cheeks of the bow roller will stop the cable from jumping out.

Riding sail

If you are sailing around the anchor, a riding sail off the backstay should help. Storm jibs tend to be a bit big for this and people whose boats are prone to career around at anchor have special riding sails made (or you can buy them off the shelf from various companies). The riding sail is set on the backstay (or either of the two backstays if you have a twin backstay set-up) and the idea is that it catches the wind and drives the stern in one direction or another and keeps it there. Riding sails are generally the preserve of the blue water sailor. Alternatively a scrap of mainsail may help.

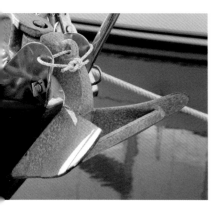

The anchor lashed to the boat

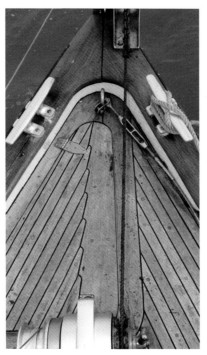

The bitter end attached to the boat by a line or lashing so it can be cut quickly

The raised ball clearly indicates to others that the vessel is at anchor

Lash the anchor

Always lash the anchor to the boat. You don't want it jumping out of its mount and setting itself unexpectedly. And always attach the bitter end to the boat but never shackle it. Tie it with a lashing or a piece of line that can be cut easily with a knife in case you need to free yourself from the anchor in a hurry.

Show that you are anchored

Always raise an anchor ball in the forepart of your vessel if anchored by day or show a riding light or anchor light at night. This tells everyone else what you are doing. You are anchored. You cannot move. They need to avoid you.

This is why it is incorrect to show an anchor light when moored to a buoy in a charted mooring area. Others expect boats to be moored there and so there is no need for the anchor light. Show your light when you are anchored because others might not necessarily expect you to be there. Added to which if someone crashed into you and you were not showing the correct signal, they might try and use this as an excuse to wriggle out of taking the blame. If you were displaying the correct signal it was clearly the other boat's fault.

USING A KEDGE ANCHOR

A kedge anchor is just a spare anchor that can deployed reasonably quickly anywhere on the boat. It can be any type of anchor – a CQR, Bruce, Delta or Spade. A Fortress anchor is popular as a kedge because it can be stowed flat and it is very powerful.

Kedging off

This is the manoeuvre from which the kedge anchor gets its name. If you have run aground on a sandbank you dinghy out an anchor and, pulling against this, winch yourself off.

Another occasion when a kedge anchor is very useful is when you're lying alongside a harbour wall and there is a degree of swell giving your fenders a real workout. If you could pull yourself off this wall things would be a good deal more comfortable.

KEDGING OFF A PONTOON OR HARBOUR WALL

- Run a bridle from bow to stern and in the middle of it (or wherever you want the main force pulling you off to be) attach a carabiner.

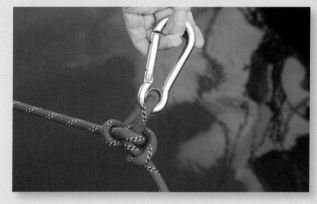

- Attach a carabiner to the bridle with an alpine butterfly knot (see box opposite).

- Now flake the cable for the kedge anchor, the chain and warp into a bucket and dinghy this out, dropping it a suitable distance off.

- Bring the bitter end back to the boat.

- Thread it through the gate of the carabiner and then up to a winch on the boat. Now winch away.

- The anchor will set and you will start to pull the boat away from the pontoon or harbour wall.

ALPINE BUTTERFLY KNOT

The alpine butterfly knot provides a secure loop in the middle of a piece of rope.
Load can be applied safely from either end of the rope or from the loop.

■ At the point in the rope that you want to tie the knot, lay the rope across the palm of the hand.

■ Take a turn around the hand to lay a second section of rope across the palm. This section has your carabiner threaded into it.

■ Now take another turn.

■ Take the top turn and bring it down to below the bottom one.

■ Then take the new top one (what was No 2) with the carabiner and bring it down below the new bottom one and up behind the other two turns.

■ Pull this out and tighten on the two parts of the rope either side and you have an alpine butterfly knot.

 Scan this QR code to watch a video on the alpine butterfly knot.

OUTBOARD MOTOR AND DINGHY

Here are a few tips about dinghy and outboard use:

- ■ Keep the prop end below the head of the outboard.

Carrying: Never lift the prop end of the outboard higher than the head because standing water in the waterways around the prop will run down the leg and corrode the bottom crank bearing. If the engine is a four-stroke make sure to lie it down on its correct side. One way will be fine, the other will allow oil to leak out. Check the manual.

- ■ Cleaning the salt water from the outboard cooling system.

Finished using the outboard? Before you take the outboard away or leave it for any time clean out the salt water from the cooling system and run the fuel out of the carburettor. To do this, stand the outboard in a bucket full of fresh water. Run it for a couple of minutes and then turn the fuel off. It will then take three minutes or so to use up the fuel in the carburettor. The engine needs to be running for about five minutes to clean the salt water out of the system. By running the fuel out of the carburettor there is no fuel in there that can congeal if left for a long time. Your outboard will last a lot longer if you keep doing this.

- ■ Fresh water rinse before packing the dinghy away.

Finished with the dinghy? If the dinghy is inflatable it will last longer if you wash it with fresh water and dry it before putting it away.

- ■ **Kill cord:** If your outboard has a kill cord always wear it when running the engine.

BAHAMIAN MOOR

This is where you set the bower anchor drop back and then set the kedge anchor off the stern and bring the boat forward so she sits between the two anchors. Then bringing the cable for the kedge anchor forward attach this to the bower cable with a rolling hitch or a swivel and let out sufficient bower cable to have the two cables drop below your keel. You now lie to these two cables and just turn with the tide around the centre, or more or less so, as the tension is taken up on one cable and then the other.

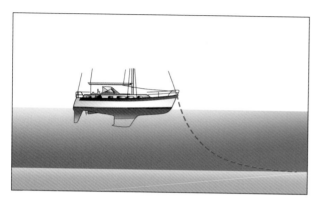

⌘ Drop and set the bower anchor.

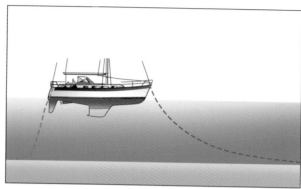

⌘ Ease back and drop and set the kedge anchor.

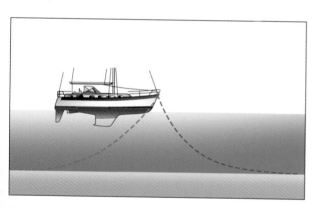

⌘ Haul in bower cable. Lying in between both anchors, attach the kedge cable to bower cable.

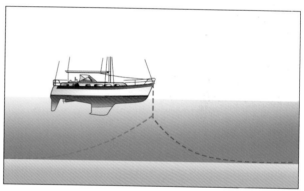

⌘ Let out enough bower cable so that the join is under the keel.

Webbing anchor cable on a drum is becoming popular. You can attach the drum to the back rail ready to deploy. It is much easier to handle than an all-chain cable and reduces any damage to varnished toe rails. I would still advocate using 10m of chain from kedge anchor to the webbing to make sure that the anchor sets and holds. I would stow the chain separately and attach it to the anchor and the webbing warp when I needed to ready the anchor.

Anchoring just off the beach with a line ashore

A LINE ASHORE

Anchoring just off the beach and taking a line ashore is very popular. I find it easier to take all the line ashore with me in the dinghy, as opposed to attaching it to the boat and paying it out as I motor or row to the shore. On shore, attach it to something immovable and then bring the line back to the boat.

GROUNDING THE BOWS ON THE BEACH

Many Mediterranean beaches are fairly shallow until a short way from the shore when they drop steeply. This allows you to drive the bow on to the beach and ground it, while the keel is in deeper water. Where this is possible, arrive bows-to and drop the kedge anchor, ground the bow, step ashore and lay out your bower anchor on the beach. Then pull back on the kedge anchor so the boat is afloat with only a few inches clearance at the bow. If there is any slight swell the bow will dig a small hollow in the soft sand. This is not a good idea where any degree of swell is expected, but there are sheltered spots where this works well.

ANCHOR STUCK?

If you can't get the anchor because it is caught on something, try driving the boat over the anchor. Try working the boat around and lifting the anchor from different angles.

Well-crewed boats talk about getting every man to stand at the bow and haul the cable in tight and then running aft in the hope that the buoyancy of the bow and the weight moved aft will dislodge the anchor. If you're single- or short-handed this isn't an option.

If the anchor really won't come up you will need to leave the anchor and the chain behind. As no one wants to lose these two expensive items it is worth buoying the chain, marking the spot with the MOB function on the GPS plotter, and hope that the local dive company will look kindly on you.

Tripping eye

You could also attach a tripping line to the eyelet in the crown of the anchor. This will allow you to pull the anchor out backwards if it becomes stuck. To set this up in advance suggests that you're not confident of the bottom and in that case I would do my best to avoid anchoring there. If I had to anchor in an emergency I might set a tripping line as a precaution. I already have an emergency; I don't need another emergency when I find I can't get my anchor out.

Any teaching aid I have ever seen that refers to tripping lines shows the buoy floating on the water above the anchor. Marking your anchor this way can be a very good thing – it might keep anyone else from laying their anchor cable over yours.

Grounding the bows on the (non-tidal) beach, with the keel in deeper water

This anchor has been set up with a tripping line

**TOP
TIP**

The contour of the land tells us what type of beach we can expect. Cliffs to the water will very likely keep going down vertically so there will be very deep water close to the shore. The land sloping gradually to the beach will give a gradually shelving beach shallow water closer to the shore.

WEATHER

Let's assume that we understand weather pretty well. If not there are many excellent books available. *Instant Weather Forecasting* by Alan Watts, as used by Bernard Moitessier, is one. Here are a few reminders though, which will keep us on the straight and narrow:

- Warm air rises. Warm air rising takes weight off the ground and therefore reduces the pressure.
- Cold air falls. Cold air falling adds weight to the ground and increases the pressure.
- Warm air holds more water than cold air.

- Warm air cools as it rises. When it cools to a certain degree the water vapour in the air condenses out as cloud. When it cools even further this water vapour condenses out as droplets of rain or ice. The temperature at this point is called the dew point.
- Cold air moves faster than warm air.
- Wind wants to blow from high pressure to low pressure, but is deflected by the Coriolis force and by friction from the ground. So the gradient wind blows more or less parallel to the isobars – at right angles to the pressure gradient.

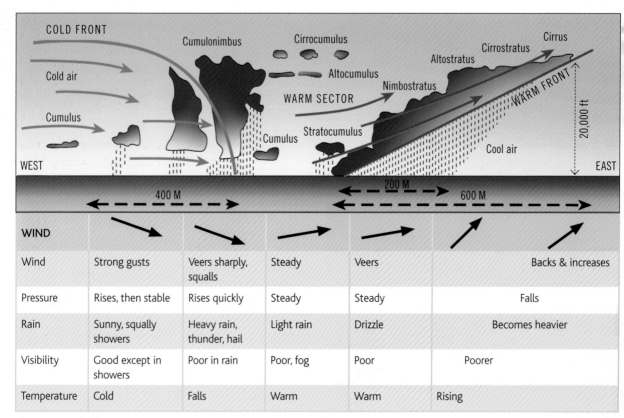

WIND						
Wind	Strong gusts	Veers sharply, squalls	Steady	Veers	Backs & increases	
Pressure	Rises, then stable	Rises quickly	Steady	Steady	Falls	
Rain	Sunny, squally showers	Heavy rain, thunder, hail	Light rain	Drizzle	Becomes heavier	
Visibility	Good except in showers	Poor in rain	Poor, fog	Poor	Poorer	
Temperature	Cold	Falls	Warm	Warm	Rising	

The passage of a depression

⌘ A sunny day is a result of cold air falling – high pressure. With cold air falling, the skies are clear and the sun is able to warm up the ground and we have a warm sunny day. At night it will cool quickly and we will notice the coolness of the cold air falling.

⌘ Cloud on a sunny day? The sun has warmed the ground, a parcel of warm moist air has risen and cooled and condensed out as cloud.

⌘ A cloudy, rainy day is a result of warm moist air rising – low pressure. Warm moist air rises and cools. The vapour condenses out as cloud. If it cools further this cloud reaches the dew point and droplets of rain are formed or perhaps ice. At night being overcast the ground is unable to radiate its heat as it would if the sky had been clear and being overcast we have warm air rising and so the night air is not so cold.

⌘ Cirrus cloud is the highest level of cloud; it has been beaten up by a great deal of wind and is whispy. Cirrus invariably tells us that a depression is on the way.

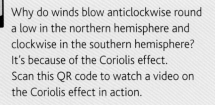

Why do winds blow anticlockwise round a low in the northern hemisphere and clockwise in the southern hemisphere? It's because of the Coriolis effect. Scan this QR code to watch a video on the Coriolis effect in action.

? A halo round the moon or sun?

This is caused by high cirrus clouds which contain ice crystals. The halo effect is the light refracting through the crystals. It may be a lovely day, but a depression is on the way.

FRONTAL SYSTEMS

A low pressure system (also known as cyclone or depression) has warm air rising, winds rushing into it and converging. A high pressure system (also known as anti-Cyclone) has cold air falling, winds rushing out of it and diverging. The key to forecasting the weather is to look at the synoptic charts, to look at the sky and to monitor the pressure. And to keep doing this until we can match up what we are seeing with what the synoptic charts are telling us.

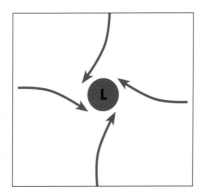

A low: warm air rising, winds converge

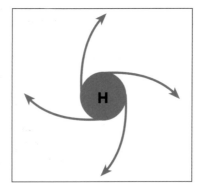

A high: cold air falling, winds diverge

WIND DIRECTION AND FRONTS IN THE NORTHERN HEMISPHERE

Warm front	Wind backs before the front and then veers as it goes through and strengthens
Mid front	Wind direction stays steady
Cold front	As the front goes through the wind veers sharply
Occluded fronts	Wind veers as the front goes through

Buys Ballot's Law says that with the wind to your back the low will be on your left (in the northern hemisphere); the high will therefore be to your right. In the southern hemisphere this is reversed.

Isobars
When the isobars are close together, it will be windy and rainy. When they are further apart, it will be sunny and less windy. Even during the passage of a depression there will be areas with sunshine; just look for a widening of the isobars.

WIND ON LAND AND SEA

When wind blows over the sea, it backs by 15° as a result of friction. Overland, wind backs by 30° as a result of friction.

Converging and diverging wind
Wind blowing parallel to a coastline where the sea is to the left of the land will be stronger; the wind on the land

Adiabatic lapse rate

This is the rate at which air cools as it rises. Dry air cools at 10°C every 1000m it rises. Moist or saturated air cools at the rate of 5.5°C every 1000m it rises.

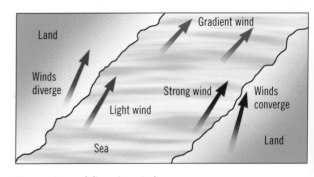

Converging and diverging winds

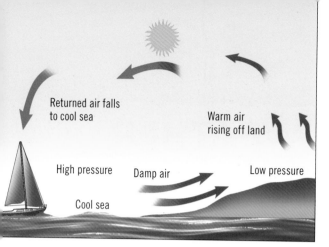

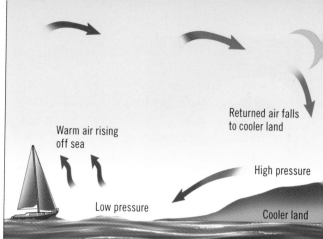

Sea breeze. The sun warms the ground. The air above is warmed and rises. As it cools the water vapour inside condenses out as cloud

Land breeze

is backed by 30° and the wind over the sea is backed by 15° so they are converging. Conversely, wind blowing parallel to a coastline where the sea is to the right of the land will be weaker as the two are diverging. This is worth bearing in mind when crossing the Channel. With a south-westerly wind, the wind near the French coast will be stronger than the predicted gradient wind and wind near the English coast will be weaker than the predicted gradient wind.

Sea breeze

The sun heats the land. The air rises, resulting in low pressure on the land. The colder air from the sea, which is at a higher pressure than the rising air on the land, blows towards the land. The warm land air that has risen to 5 miles or so is blown out to sea. It cools and so it falls, maintaining the higher pressure over the sea. This carries on until either the heat source, the sun, stops warming up the land or until an opposing gradient wind is strong enough to cancel out the sea breeze. A south-westerly sea breeze will be cancelled out by a north-easterly gradient wind, for example.

Land breeze

When the sun sets the land cools and now the pressure difference changes. The land has lower air pressure than the sea and so the sea breeze effect is reversed and wind blows from the land out to sea.

▶ *Crossed winds rule*

Crossed winds rule

If you stand with your back to the wind and the upper wind or rather the clouds move across you from left to right, then the weather will deteriorate. You are in front of the depression. If you stand with your back to the wind and the upper wind or clouds come from right to left the weather will improve. You are at the back of or behind the low. Again, this is reversed in the southern hemisphere where you'd be facing the wind.

You can apply this rule to what you are experiencing in terms of pressure wind strength and weather:

- In front of a warm front (clouds moving across from left to right) the pressure will have dropped, it will be raining and the wind will have increased in strength.
- At the cold front (clouds moving across from right to left) the pressure will be rising, you will have squally showers, but there will be gaps of blue in the sky as the weather is improving.

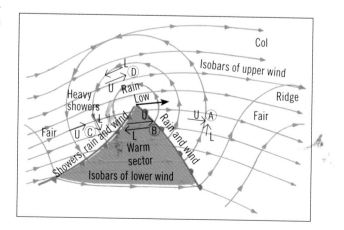

HEAVY WEATHER SAILING STRATEGY

Although I don't like glib aphorisms, 'If in doubt don't go out' does make sense. It's true, we know how to get off the dock in more or less any condition. We know how to get on the dock in more or less any condition. We know how to match the sails to the wind and sea conditions and to put that reef in before we go out. We know how to heave to. So we know how to do everything we might need to do to go out in heavy weather. But do we really want to go if we don't have to? Probably not.

Passagemakers and blue water sailors don't have any choice when it comes to heavy weather, they just have to face it. But weekend and holiday sailors can choose. We can decide that the conditions forecast are more than we want to go sailing in. Interestingly, Lin and Larry Pardey, who have sailed more than 200,000 miles over the past 45 years (past all the great southern capes and twice around), said that storms accounted for less than 2% of their passagemaking. Eric Hiscock, who made three circumnavigations with his wife Susan, said that the average wind speed during his world cruising life had been 10–12 knots.

There is one important thing to understand, though: If you do decide to go out in heavy weather you will discover the difference between a landsman and a sailor. For a landsman the land is safe and the sea is dangerous. For a sailor the sea is safe and the land is dangerous. You could go out in heavy weather and find that returning to port was dangerous, a lee shore, breaking waves at the entrance and so forth, and that staying at sea until conditions had improved was the safest option.

So before setting off, check the forecast to make sure that returning to harbour is likely to be an option. Even relatively low wind speeds with opposing tides can make things very uncomfortable; 20 knots of wind against a strongly ebbing tide in shallow water or over a bar will make the conditions rough. There is a mass of weather data available to help you decide what it will be like out there and local knowledge is always worth listening to. You should always know what to expect before you set off.

Remember that you are single-handed or short-handed and will get tired quickly in heavy weather – so prepare a strategy for coping with it. Preparation, the key to stress-free sailing, is never more important than when facing heavy weather. Nature has upped the ante. Where you might have been able to tame a sheet that has slipped off the winch, now with strong winds the sheet will lash about dangerously. Lines are now bar taut and the boat comes under a great deal of tension, which is why it is time to reduce gear and shorten sail. I find hanging on very tiring and the motion of the boat mind-numbing so I have carefully prepared strategies and systems to use in these circumstances.

Not a day to go for a sail

A trysail

USING THE RIGHT SAILS

Getting the best out of heavy weather means having
the correctly shaped sails for the conditions. Roller-
furling headsails, which are a fabulous convenience in
moderate weather, now become a bit of a liability. The
shape of the sail which is perfect when it is fully set
becomes less successful the more it is reefed. If you are
going to sail in all weathers you will have a suit of sails
– No 1 genoa, lapper (135–140%), No 2, No 3 and a
storm jib – so you can match the sail to the occasion.
I have just such a selection and will set the correct sail
on the furler for the expected wind strength. My storm
jib hanks on to a removable inner forestay, which I set
up when necessary.

A mainsail to match the foresails should have at
least two reefs, preferably three reefs, after which you
would move to a trysail. A trysail really needs its own
track so that you can set it in place before it gets too
blowy and then tie it down ready for when you might
need it.

CENTRING THE EFFORT

The ideal when it comes to reducing sail is to bring
the centre of effort inboard, as this helps to balance
the boat. As a main is reefed there is less sail aft
and therefore less effort aft. If you had a jib set on a
bowsprit and a staysail you would hand the jib to move
the effort inboard.

*I get away with being able to feed my trysail into the gate for
the main track because the header on my main tucks down just
under the gate. This is not always the case on every boat and
it does mean that it has already started to blow up when I am
setting the trysail, which is not ideal*

Storm jib hanked on to a removable inner forestay

With a single forestay you can only reduce the amount of sail set and cannot move its effort inboard until you set a storm jib. For boats with only a single forestay and roller furling it's a good idea to have a removable forestay for the storm jib; this can be stored by the shrouds and, when needed, set to a D-ring in the deck and tensioned with a highfield lever, tackle, turning block or bottle screw. Check that the storm jib has been cut so that your existing sheet leads will work with it.

Whatever system or set of sails you have it is important to go out and test them in benign conditions. It is no good finding that when it comes to setting up the inner forestay for the storm job that you are missing a vital shackle.

The old saying that if you think you should reef, you should do so immediately is absolutely true. Because if you wait and the wind strengthens reefing will be harder. If the wind eases, it will be easy to shake the reef out.

BALANCING THE SAILS

An important part of heavy weather sailing is balancing the sails. If the headsail overpowers the mainsail it is hard to get the bow of the boat through the wind when you tack because you lose the momentum of the turn as the headsail is beaten down by the wind. Reduce the size of the headsail and you will be able to tack. Once the wind reaches a certain strength it is possible to sail to windward without a headsail at all as there is sufficient windage in the bow of the boat. Indeed, at 30 knots and above you can heave to with a triple-reefed main and no headsail.

WEATHER HELM

There are two dynamic forces at work on a boat: the aerodynamic force from the wind in the sails and the hydrodynamic force from the water over the keel. Each of these forces has a centre point; when they are in line the boat is balanced. If the centre of the aerodynamic force moves behind the centre of the hydrodynamic force the boat will round up into the wind and you will experience weather helm. This means that when the boat is trying to round up into the wind you have to try to steer it to bring the bow down by bringing the helm up to windward (ie to weather).

If the forces are the other way round, with the aerodynamic force forward of the hydrodynamic one, the boat will fall off to leeward and present her stern to the wind. This is undesirable since any boat that, left unattended, could fall off to leeward and run downwind is leaving herself open to a crash gybe. So you want a boat to have a degree of weather helm so that she will luff up if left alone but not so much weather helm that you have to fight it all the time.

As the wind strength increases you will experience more weather helm. Reduce the sail area to reduce the weather helm and then balance the sails to make sure that the main isn't overpowering the headsail. There are many things you can do to reduce the power in the main: flatten the sail by tensioning the foot on the clew outhaul and sheeting in, open the leech, drop the main car to leeward or, indeed, reef. Or you can increase the power of the headsail.

Of course, there is an exception to every rule and a popular first step in reducing sail for a ketch is to drop the main, leaving just the headsail and the mizzen. This is called running under 'jib and jigger'

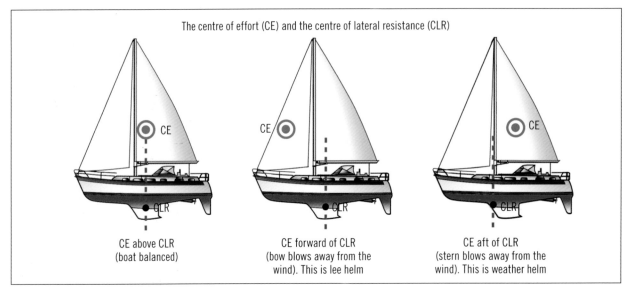

The centre of effort (CE) and the centre of lateral resistance (CLR)

| CE above CLR (boat balanced) | CE forward of CLR (bow blows away from the wind). This is lee helm | CE aft of CLR (stern blows away from the wind). This is weather helm |

Lee helm and weather helm

Generally speaking, in strong winds it will be a question of balancing the amount of mainsail with the amount of headsail. The more you reef the main the more you bring the centre of effort forward and reduce weather helm. Finding the sweet spot is something you can practise.

SETTING THE BOAT UP FOR HEAVY WEATHER

Deck equipment
Make sure everything is lashed down: anchor lashed to the bow roller, spinnaker poles, liferaft and dinghies secured. A liferaft canister will have a quick-release mechanism to release its securing straps (which might be a pelican clip or a hydrostatic release), but the heavy liferaft must still be well secured to the deck or its cradle. Any rigid dinghies also need to be well secured, while inflatables should be deflated and stowed. Boathooks and brushes on deck can be fastened to the grab rails with bungees.

Hatches
Check that they are all closed and secured. Anyone in the forward cabin may have cracked the hatch to get a little air and not have closed it. It's worth checking because they certainly won't be having a good night's sleep if their bedding gets wet.

Washboards
You'll need a washboard policy; this will differ from boat to boat and point of sail. A displacement boat running before a heavy sea will want all the washboards in place and the hatch closed in case any water comes in over the stern. A centre cockpit boat sailing to windward in the same sea may not need any washboards in at all. All you are doing here is playing safe. It is an incredible faff to have to take the washboards out every time you want to go below or come up into the cockpit. A few boats will have just one washboard, most will have two and some will have more (for example *Elinor*, our test Contessa 26, had many washboards, each about four inches across). You only need to put washboards in when there is a danger that a wave will land in the cockpit, either from forward as it sweeps down the boat or from astern.

Life jackets
The RYA recommends that you wear a life jacket at all times unless you feel that it is safe not to do so. So that covers the RYA when it comes to anyone taking them to court and puts the onus squarely on us. But it does give us choice and stacks up with the RYA mantra of 'education rather than legislation'. And, of course, the wearing of life jackets is a context thing. The RNLI advertisement simply says 'useless unless worn'.

Lifelines

You can prevent yourself from going over the side in the first instance by holding on. Then, as a safety measure, you can wear a lifeline. I wear a life jacket and clip my lifeline to this. Others may simply wear a harness and clip the lifeline to that. If you are in the middle of the ocean and single-handing you don't really need or want a life jacket, but you may want to be clipped on to the boat so a harness is generally preferred.

One thing to remember about lifelines is that they are generally too long. The lifeline on my boat started out as 1.96m fully extended and, when clipped on to the jack stay and taken over the top guard rail, would stretch to the water. With my weight on the end of this that would put my head up to a foot under water. It wouldn't take long with the boat going at 6 knots for me to drown. So we need lifelines that are as short as possible; about 93cm is right for me. You only need enough length to be able to stand at the mast. So I tied a knot in my lifeline to shorten it. Now the lifeline doesn't stretch so far and there is a good chance I won't be dragged underwater if I go over the guardwire.

If you plan to unclip from one thing and then clip on to something else then you either need to use two lifelines so that you are always tethered to one strong point while you set up the tether to the next, or you need to use lifelines with three carabiners, one at either end and one in the middle, for just this purpose.

In heavy weather with a boat bouncing around a bit it is always a good idea to clip on in the cockpit. Check how far you would go with the full length of lifeline if attached to a D-ring in the cockpit sole and if this looks likely to have you over the side, shorten it. Boats with aft cockpits and no sprayhoods where you are fully exposed to the weather make crew very well aware of how vulnerable they are and the need to clip on. Centre cockpit boats with sprayhoods and a good degree of protection from the conditions can give you a false sense of security. It is easy to get bounced out of a cockpit. Me? I clip on.

Jackstays and strong points

Check your jackstays for chafe and give. The less give the better. Check your strong points. All of these may have to take the strain of a heavy person being thrown overboard.

My shortened lifeline allows me to stand at the mast comfortably

Handholds

Do you have good stout handholds on the boat where you need them? I have been on boats where from stepping out of the cockpit until you're by the mast there isn't a decent handhold. My own boat could do with a handhold on the side of the windscreen. If you aren't sure where you might need handholds a walk around the boat while out in a bit of sea and wind will soon tell you.

Prepare the storm jib and trysail

Check out the storm jib and the trysail on the dock. Set them up and make sure you have all the kit you need. If you know how to do it on the dock there is a good chance you will know how to do it when you need to. Then practise in 30 knots of wind.

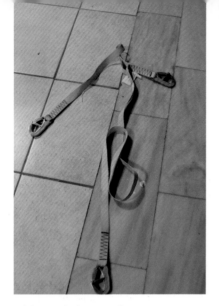

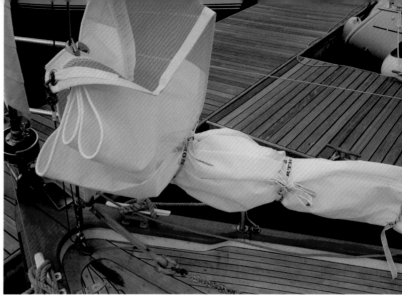

Lifeline with three carabiners

Practise using the storm jib on the dock

Secure below

Everything below should be properly stowed. Imagine the boat heeled over hard on either side: can anything fly out of a shelf or locker? If so, secure it.

- **Lockers and cupboards:** Secure with an X of gaffer tape.
- **Drawers:** Secure with bungees or ties.
- **Doors:** Secure with latches if they are liable to fly open.
- **Floorboards:** I have never seen any cruising boat with securing devices for these, but blue water sailors will always be able to lock down their floorboards.
- **Bunks/berths with lockers under:** The same goes for these. Blue water sailors will have straps for these.
- **Cooker:** Check that there is a bar to stop it from jumping out of its gymbals. Most cookers would fall out if the boat were laid on its beam ends, not to mention inverted.
- **Lee cloths:** You need to be able to secure yourself in a safe berth when the boat is moving about and you're riding out a storm so lee cloths fitted to the saloon or quarter berths are important.

Clothing and warmth

Once you have become cold and wet, it is incredibly difficult to become warm and dry again. So if you can keep warm and dry, so much the better. This means having the proper gear. I even have some nice scuba diving goggles, not because I intend to sail the southern ocean, but simply because if there is salt water flying about or sideways rain it is a lot easier on the eyes to pop the goggles on if I need to do a stint on the helm. I am not going to win any fashion show, that's for certain, but then as I am on my own, who will see?

Food

It is possibly obvious, but with a boat that is moving around a bit not many people will be inclined to go below and cook. It's therefore a good idea to prepare as much food in advance of heavy weather as you can manage. Hot drinks and soup from thermos flasks are incredibly welcome when you are being beaten up by a heavy sea.

Locker secured with gaffer tape

▲ *Latched door*

◀ *Drawers secured with a bungee cord*

▲ *With there being a gap between the wings of the gimbal bracket there is a chance that the cooker would fly off its mountings if the boat were inverted*

Filters *i*

When the boat is being tossed about, sediment in any tank will be stirred up and will be caught by the filters on the various pumps, which will eventually block. So you need to know how to change or clean them. Discovering how to do this while attached to the dock is a lot less exciting than doing it at sea.

Just a thought here: don't make everything too hot. The thermos flask will retain the heat and there is nothing worse than trying to drink something that is scalding you. In heavy weather it is not really an option to pour some out into a cup and allow it to cool down; much better to be able to pour it into a cup and drink it straight away.

Rest

Heavy weather is tiring and so you need to get as much rest as you can to be as fresh as possible when you have to do something on deck.

Navigation

You need to have planned your navigation before the heavy weather sets in. Again, no one is going to want to go below and start reading almanacs, plotting waypoints or writing on a chart when the boat is moving about a lot.

Sea room

Land is incredibly dangerous stuff for boats. When the sea becomes rough we have to remind ourselves that while we may be tossing about rather alarmingly and uncomfortably, it is safer being here at sea than being near the land because the land is what will shipwreck us. So we need sea room; room to drift with the tide and the wind.

A harbour to weather is best

If you don't like the idea of being out in heavy weather, you should stay in harbour having read the weather forecast and not go out. But if you have gone out and perhaps the weather is worse than expected from the forecast, you have to be very careful about returning. There are many all-weather harbours, but even so it is not always safe to enter them. Approaching a harbour to weather will be safer than approaching a downwind harbour on a lee shore. Also, despite the fact that it is hard-going beating up to the weather harbour, the closer you get the easier it becomes as the land should afford you some shelter.

Bosun's bag

Have a bosun's bag of a knife, essential screwdrivers (slotted and cross head) and any other useful tools ready. Know where the bolt cutters are. Sometimes bolt cutters work on rigging that needs to be cut away; sometimes a screwdriver is more useful.

VERY HEAVY WEATHER

How can we manage in very heavy weather? Everyone should have a very heavy weather strategy. There are a number of books worth reading that cover this in detail. Peter Bruce's *Heavy Weather Sailing* is an excellent compendium of experiences from racing and cruising sailors, the strategies they employed, what worked and what didn't.

Racing yachts are fond of running before the sea. They are racing, they want to keep going and they have a number of very fit people on board. And they need to have them because it is very tiring helming a boat before a sea. About half an hour at the helm is enough before you need a break. Some lie a-hull. Others stream drogues or warps to slow their progress. Some trail all their anchor chain and the anchor.

Each to their own, but the difficulty with running is that you need plenty of sea room, you lose all the ground you had made to windward and you need a good strong crew. Added to which there is always the risk of broaching or being pitch poled (as famously happened to the Smeetons in *Tzu Hang*).

Lying a-hull means you don't have to do anything but the boat does lie beam on to the sea which leaves you open to being rolled and the motion is very uncomfortable.

As for trailing warps and ground tackle, well, I am not sure. Studying the experts, those who have travelled hundreds of thousands of miles across oceans and who have experience of riding out storms, I have come to the conclusion that there are two excellent survival options:

1. The Series Drogue as designed by Don Jordan. This comprises a leather bridle, a leader, a tapered line with 5-inch cones attached and then a weighted chain at the end. Between 100 and 200 cones are used depending on the length of the line which is matched to the displacement of the vessel. This Jordan Series Drogue is then trailed from the stern and slows the boat to between 2 to 3 knots. The crew strap themselves in below and ride out the storm. Points to note: it is very easy to deploy, but there are a number of stories about how difficult it is to retrieve. In defence, the makers say that retrieval is straightforward, but that it has to

be done correctly. For this method it is important to have washboards that are stout and will not let water get below and a cockpit that drains quickly, because there is every chance that a wave or two will come in over the stern.

2. The Lin and Larry Pardey technique where they heave to with a parachute anchor to hold them. This is described in their book *Storm Tactics*, which I consider to be the bible when it comes to heavy weather strategy. Don't confuse this technique with simply lying to a parachute anchor, because with the Pardey technique of heaving to and using the parachute anchor to hold the boat at an angle to the wind and sea, they create a slick as the boat drifts back. Somehow this slick to windward has the 'ability to break the power of the seas'. So it is extremely important to lie within this slick, stopped in the water. For their 30-foot boat, they deploy an 8-foot parachute anchor from the bow. They let out 250 feet of line so that the parachute is one wavelength away, so that while they are on the crest of a wave the parachute is on the crest of the next wave. They then have a bridle which is attached by a snatch block to the line and runs back to a cockpit winch and this they use to help adjust the angle they make to the wind and waves. This holds their boat perfectly within her slick. The waves lose their power before they reach the boat and they can comfortably ride out the storm. Their rate of drift is less than 1 knot.

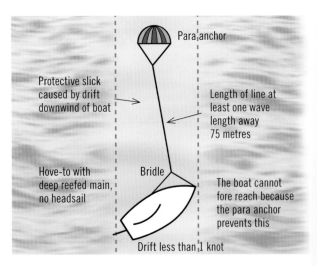

Heaving to under para anchor

The Pardeys say that deployment and retrieval are not difficult. They don't weight the parachute anchor and they don't use trip lines for the retrieval. They just winch it in when things have calmed down. They also say that not a drop of water comes aboard when they lie like this in a storm.

I haven't been out in survival conditions yet, but when I do go I will be armed with a parachute anchor, having practised a great deal before I go.

WHEN TO HEAVE TO

- **Close-hauled:** When the seas start to hit the windward bow and it becomes uncomfortable it's time.
- **Beam reach:** Again, heave to when the waves become uncomfortable.
- **Running:** When the waves start breaking under the transom, when we feel as if we are being thrown forward by the waves and the helm loses steerage is the time to heave to. Now you have to be careful because to heave to you need to round up and this means presenting your beam to the seas. Timing is key here. Drop the headsail and time your rounding up between the breaking seas as close to the waves to leeward as possible, sheeting in the main as you round up. Avoid going beam on to a big sea.

One of my students who worked for a management consultancy firm came up with the following acronym when setting off into heavy weather: REEFAPLC.

R = Reef before you set off
E = Establish a safe bolt hole
E = Ensure all crew are wearing warm clothes and wet weather gear
F = Food, prepare in advance
A = Advise coastguard of a shore contact
P = Plan navigation in advance
L = Life jacket and lifelines
C = Check bilges, deck gear, hatches, stow for sea

Well, it kept the class amused.

Checking out the tri sail on a lovely day

10 NAVIGATION

If you are short-handed or even single-handed all the navigation will be down to you alone or to share with one other crew. Piloting the boat in confined waters will require identification of marks and lights, monitoring the depth sounder and helming and you will have had to plan your approach to any harbour beforehand.

Of course, you will use your GPS chart plotter all the time. You'd be mad not to. It gives you your position to within 2 metres 24/7 – fantastic. You can even put the bearing to your waypoint into the plotter, the time of day and date and it will tell you (at least some of them) what course you need to steer to allow for the tide. You can adjust that for leeway and you're off. Always keep a paper plot just in case, as your safety margin.

But whatever your chart plotter tells you, you will still need to be able to confirm by eye that the mark you're supposed to be approaching is indeed the mark you're looking for. You can use the chart plotter for establishing distances and bearings to and from various things or you can do this on your paper chart, but there are also useful age-old techniques to give you an instant indication of angles and distances. I'll mention some of these handy shortcuts below.

Again, navigation and pilotage is all about preparation. Don't enter a pilotage situation without a plan. I am not the first to say it and I won't be the last, but having an easy-to-follow plan when entering a foreign harbour will take the stress out of things immeasurably. Of course, you will refer to your chart plotter to guide you, but measuring the bearings and distances from one mark to the next in advance will help you to anticipate the plotter and, if it were to fail, you wouldn't be left high and dry. So let's look at some techniques to help simplify navigation:

MEASURE WITH YOUR BODY

The body is an onboard measuring device.

An outstretched arm is a bearing line

I am always in the same position when I am on the helm on my boat so I can stretch out an arm in the direction of any vessel with which we are closing to see if we are on a constant bearing. I point at her and if she comes down my arm we will collide. If she goes ahead of my arm I'm going astern of her and if she drops back from my arm I'm going ahead of her. You can also line up a stanchion and a winch, anything really. And standing behind the binnacle compass I can match my arm to the bearing I need. The buoy bears 135°. Noting where 135° is on the compass and pointing my arm in that direction, I should see the buoy.

Using an outstretched arm as a bearing line

Fingers are degrees of angles

One finger at arm's length represents 2° at the horizon. So if you are aiming at a headland on the horizon and you want to know how much to alter course in order to clear it you can use one of the four measuring devices available on your hand, from 2° to 20°. If you want to measure how much to alter course to avoid a buoy which is not actually on the horizon then just bend your elbow a bit and bring your hand or finger closer to you and work with this. Bringing your hand closer to your face allows this rough calculation to work for obstacles that are closer to you. And I can do that quicker than I can move the plotter cursor to give me an accurate bearing. There is always an 'ish' factor to all navigation out on the water, of course.

⌘ 1 finger = 2°

⌘ 2 fingers = 4°

⌘ 3 fingers = 6°

⌘ 4 fingers = 8°

⌘ 5 fingers = 10°

⌘ This is 20°

Watch the background

If there is a background behind the vessel you're monitoring then as long as that is changing you will miss her. If she is eating up the background ahead of her and spitting it out astern she is going ahead of you. If the background is opening out ahead of her and being eaten up by her stern you're going ahead of her. If it is static and you are closing, you are going to collide.

DISTANCES

Standing in the cockpit of a 35-foot sailing boat your distance to the horizon is roughly 3.5 miles. You can calculate this in two ways:

- 2.08 x square root of height of eye in metres = miles to the horizon.
- 1.15 x square root of height of eye in feet = miles to the horizon.

Say your height of eye is 9 feet (from the water), which is 2.74 metres, then method 1 gives us 2.08 x $\sqrt{2.74}$m (1.66) = 3.45 miles and method 2 gives us 1.15 x $\sqrt{9}$ft (3) = 3.45 miles.

Of course, I can't do complicated square roots or multiply by 2.08 in my head and even multiplying by 1.15 gives me pause for thought, so I simplify things. I will multiply by 2 for metres (not 2.08) and by 1.2 for feet (not 1.15). So there will be an 'ish' factor to it, but as long as I allow myself a margin of safety then I will be fine. Essentially a 6-foot man standing at the helm of an average 35-foot boat will have a distance to the horizon of about 3.5 miles.

The 'one in sixty' rule

The figure 60 is very important in navigation. In time we have 60 seconds in a minute and 60 minutes in an hour. On the chart we then have 60' in 1°. And we use 60 in a number of ways. The 'one in sixty' rule is based around the fact that if you have a right-angle triangle and the longest side measures 60 units then the length of the shortest side will be the same in units as the degrees of the angle opposite.

So if the angle opposite the shortest side is 2°, the length of the shortest side will be 2 units. If you travel for 60 miles and you're off course by 3° you'll have missed your destination by 3 miles. And you can play with this and pro rate it. Travelled for 30 miles and off course by 5°? Then you will miss your destination by 2.5 miles. If you had travelled 60 miles you'd have missed it by 5 miles, but you only travelled half as far (30 miles) so you will miss it by half as much, ie 2.5 miles.

How far off the buoy?

And we can use the one in sixty rule for all sorts of things. You're passing a buoy or a headland: how far off it are you? Take a bearing of the buoy when it is

2.08 × √Ht of eye in metres = distance in miles

1.15 × √Ht of eye in feet = distance in miles

Distance to the horizon

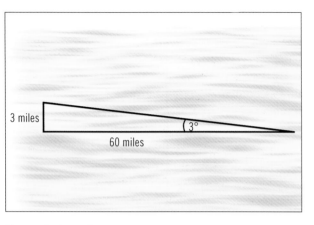

The one in sixty rule

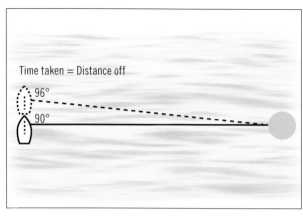

How far off are you?

abeam, say that is 90°. Now maintain your course and time how many minutes it takes for the bearing of the buoy to change by the same number of degrees as your speed over the ground. And that time will be your distance off. Say you are doing 6 knots over the ground and it takes 2 min and 30 seconds for the bearing on the buoy to change from 90° to 96°, then your distance off will be 2.5 miles. That's handy and you can do that in your head – well, as long as you have a hand-bearing compass and a watch.

Apparent to true

Not everyone has digital wind speed and direction readouts that give true wind speed and direction at the press of a button. I, for one, have instruments that give me apparent wind speed and direction data only. We know that when we move through the water we bring the wind direction towards the bow and if we are sailing to windward apparently increase it.

However, if you want the true data you can simply work this out on a piece of paper.

Spectacle deviation

Check that your reading or day glasses do not deviate your hand-bearing compass. Given that we usually use the hand-bearing compass to give us the deviation of the ship's compass, knowing that the hand-bearing compass is giving us a correct magnetic reading is important.

And that's another thought: always check the ship's compass of any new boat you step on to. Many's the time I have spotted deviation of up to 30° of the ship's compass just because an owner has forgotten to allow for this when they added that new electronic gizmo slap bang next to the ship's magnetic compass.

▶ *Glasses can deviate a hand-bearing compass*

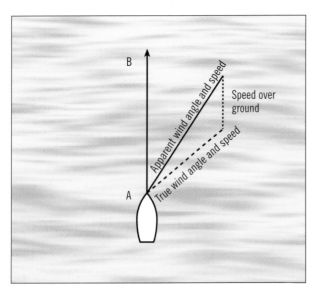

Apparent to true wind conversion

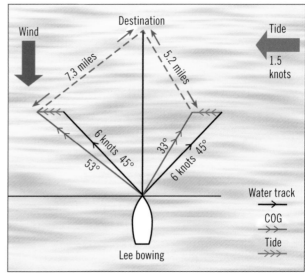

Lee bowing

Draw a line A–B. Your boat is at A. A–B is your heading. From A draw in the angle of your apparent wind. Draw this line to a scale that matches the apparent wind speed. Say apparent wind speed is 10 knots, then the line could be 10cm long. At the end of the line draw a line back, parallel to the A–B line to the value in these units of your speed over the ground, say 6 knots, so 6cm. Where this ends, join it up with your boat at A. The angle of this line is then the angle of the true wind and the length of the line in units is the speed of the true wind. Working from true to apparent you'd reverse the process. Simple, who needs a digital readout? Digital readouts are handy, although sometimes I think working through the process gives us a greater understanding of things.

LEE BOWING

It is always worth being aware of the effect of lee bowing and to use it to your advantage:

- Tide on the lee bow will push the boat up to windward.
- Tide on the windward bow will push the boat to leeward.

Assuming your destination is to windward you want to get there as directly as possible. By choosing the tack that puts the tide on the lee bow, the tide pushing the boat to windward results in a freeing effect – the apparent wind is brought aft and strengthened – and you are able to sail closer to the wind than if the tide were on your windward bow. The effect can be quite dramatic.

Let's say we sail at 45° to the wind, making 6 knots through the water with a cross tide of 1.5 knots. By lee bowing on port tack we can sail closer to the wind at 33°. On starboard with the tide on our windward side our 45° becomes 53°. At the end of an hour we would find that the distance to our destination when on port was 5.2 miles whereas the distance to our destination on starboard was greater at 7.3 miles.

You need to keep an eye on things to make sure that you don't get caught out by any wind shifts or changes in the tidal stream, but if you consider lee bowing you can take the stress out of things by avoiding the tack that will take you well off course and significantly downtide. You always want to arrive at your destination slightly uptide. You can always free off and let the tide take you down to your destination. It is a lot harder to make up the ground to get back uptide.

Velocity made good is simply the speed you are making towards your destination. When you're sailing

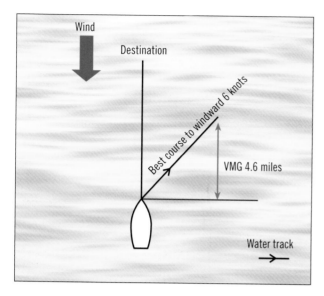

Velocity made good

Tacking up the cone

to windward you will have to tack your way there. Velocity made good is the rate of progress to your destination per hour.

Tacking up the cone

Your destination is to windward so you will have to tack there. Rather than make long tacks in each direction, you can tack up a cone that spreads out 15° either side of the destination. That way you won't end up miles from your destination just as the wind makes an unfavourable shift. You also need to keep an eye out for favourable wind shifts. And, of course, if there is any cross tide you can always lee bow.

MOON PHASES

Knowing the state of the tide just by looking at the phase of the moon is very handy. When you see a D shape in the sky the moon is waxing, going from a new moon (springs) to a full moon (springs). A perfect D indicates a neap tide, more or less. When you see a C shape the moon is waning.

And no matter where we are in the world, HW springs at our home port will be at the same time, +/- 1 hour, every time, while HW neaps will be about 6 hours different, +/- 1 hour, every time. In

Southampton HW springs is roughly speaking at 1200 and 0000, neaps at 0600 and 1800. In Plymouth HW springs is roughly at 0700 and 1900, with neaps at 0100 and 1300.

Tides advance roughly 50 minutes in every 24 hours. So HW this morning at 1100 means HW tomorrow will be at 1150. Without looking at a tide table if I see a full moon I know HW Southampton is roughly 1200 and so HW three days hence, say, will be roughly at 1430 (4 x 50 = 150 min). High water in seven days time will, of course, be neaps and so six hours different from springs – 0600 and 1800 for Southampton.

So when I'm at home and I see a full moon I know the time of HW at my marina; if I see a crescent moon (neaps) I know what time HW will be. I also know that the pressure is higher rather than lower – clear sky as opposed to overcast – and that tells me the wind will be more northerly. Overcast, a low, will give more southerly winds. So I have a great deal of information before I even set off from home, just by looking at the sky.

If you're a Solent sailor you can add in that the tide turns an hour before HW Portsmouth and that means on a spring tide a daytime sail will take me to the west to use the tide to my advantage. Wherever you are in the world these pieces of local information affect your sailing, so keeping tabs on the moon is key.

THREE PENCIL NAVIGATION

We never really find ourselves in a position of absolutely not knowing where we are, because we will always have started from somewhere and even if the GPS has packed in we will have been keeping a paper plot and run up our dead reckoning and estimated position every hour. So we will be somewhere within a circle of uncertainty. But if the worst came to the worst we could always tie three pencils together, point the bottom one roughly horizontal to the sea and adjust the one on the angle so we could sight the North Star down it. Then it's a question of sailing west or east, keeping the North Star in the same position until we hit land.

Trying this down at Cape Horn would be a bit disappointing though as there is nothing on the same latitude and the first bit of land you would hit after leaving Cape Horn would be Cape Horn.

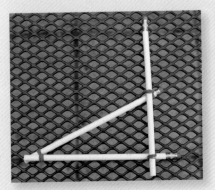

■ Three pencils arranged as a navigation aid.

■ Three pencil navigation.

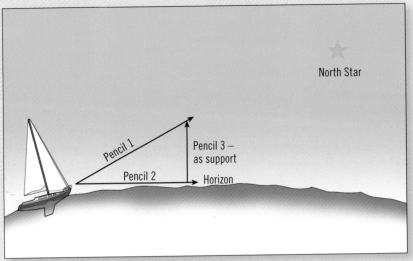

TABLET NAVIGATION

And my favourite, navigating with my tablet. Technology is moving so fast that by the time I have finished this sentence the system that I use will be out of date. For now though, running an iPad2 3G, I am able to receive true Navstar GPS information and with iNavx software (the only tablet software at present that outputs NMEA data) I am able to run my autopilot. My boat has a screen and sprayhood so my unprotected iPad can be out in most conditions. Boats with open cockpits will need to invest in a protective case.

I only linked the tablet to the autopilot for a bit of fun, but it was every bit as good as my chart plotter at running my boat. It's probably not serious competition for a chart plotter on a sailing boat, but it might be on a motor boat. My set-up cost less than half that of a plotter of comparable screen size and I could take photos on it and then send these to friends once I was in mobile/internet range. And I could shop on it and watch movies, listen to music, write stuff, pay bills...

Other electronics

I have a radar, which is useful. And you really benefit from having an Automatic Identification System receiver (AIS) if you're crossing seas with a lot of shipping. When I buy an AIS it will be a transponder so I can send my data as well as receive other people's.

Dinghy at night?

Under 7 metres going at less than 7 knots you are allowed to show a single all-round white light. In a dinghy this is usually just the torch, but here is an idea: a cap light.

Cap light used as an all-round white light on a dinghy

Stars and planets

Stars twinkle, planets don't. That's not strictly true, but near enough. Stars and planets, even the sun and the moon, all twinkle to some degree. As their light reaches us it passes through air and turbulence in the earth's atmosphere causes the light to refract differently from one moment to the next. To us the object is seen to jigger about or, as the astronomers say, 'scintillate'. The further away an object is the greater the effect. Stars are much, much, much further away than the planets, sun and moon and so they are more likely to appear to 'scintillate'.

The derivation of springs and neaps

It seems they come from the Anglo Saxon. *Springan* meaning to bulge, and *nep*, meaning lacking or lower – nothing to do with the seasons or a vegetable the Scots have with their haggis.

11 MAN OVERBOARD STRATEGY

Fortunately people don't go overboard very often. But when they do, the conditions are likely to be lively and getting back to the man overboard (MOB) and retrieving them will not be easy. It helps to have a strategy and a set-up for the retrieval of the MOB and we can practise, not just on sunny, calm days but on the sort of day when someone could fall in. Take a day with 20 knots of wind and a bit of a sea, because those are the conditions when you'll need to bring your boat to a standstill alongside the practice MOB.

There are a number of strategies taught for returning to an MOB. Some people sail round in a wide circle, tacking and gybing, others sail in a figure of eight. Others crash tack immediately and drift down on to the MOB.

As single-handers (the crew is in the water) we have to do everything. We have to sail the boat, keep watching the MOB, start the engine, ready the boathook. At night or in any sea we need to mark the area. The minute our crew goes over the side, we have to throw in anything we have to hand: lifebuoy, cushions, jackets, any polypropylene rope (since it floats). We should already have rigged a search light; I rig this and have it standing by and working on every night passage as part of my preparation. So there is a lot to do. What we don't throw in, of course, is the throwing line. We will need this when we get back to the MOB.

GETTING BACK TO THE MOB

Sailing to windward: strategy 1

Getting back to the MOB quickly, under control and being able to stop the boat by the MOB, upwind of him if conditions allow, head to wind if not, is key for me. And I do not want to be very far from the MOB at any point. So, if you're close-hauled when the MOB went in, you can employ the following strategy:

1. Bear away on to a broad reach.
2. Start the engine.
3. Crash tack.
4. Sail back to the MOB close-hauled with the headsail aback.
5. Heave to above the MOB.

◄ *This practice MOB is a buoy with a decent chunk of wrapped and knotted rope to give it a body. Using a fender and a bucket is not great for practice because if you're still making a knot or so as you try to lift the fender out of the water the resistance from the bucket being towed through the water will be enormous*

Bearing away on to a broad reach gives you a moment to think. It will level the boat for a start. If you have an engine turn it on. After all, it is much smarter to use a little help from the engine than to execute a perfect return to the the MOB under sail, over shoot him and have to go around again. And as a friend pointed out, rather morbidly: 'When they ask you at the inquest if you started the engine and you say you didn't, you will look a bit of a Charlie.'

You'll be familiar with crash tacking the boat and sailing to windward with a backed headsail from Chapter 5. You have the engine to help you here, but if it wouldn't start for some reason you'd need to rely on your skills to manoeuvre the boat and get it to stop by the MOB. In an ideal world you'll heave to stopped in the water directly above the MOB. My boat heaves to with the main near the centre. Some boats require the main to be eased.

If you're relying on the engine to hold station then letting the main right out and allowing it to luff is a good idea. This is something you should check and practise, as each boat will be different. Make sure you can hold the boat stopped in the water by the MOB whether hove to alone or under engine with main set. Usual rules regarding engines and dangly legs apply: engine in neutral when the MOB is close to the boat and abaft the beam.

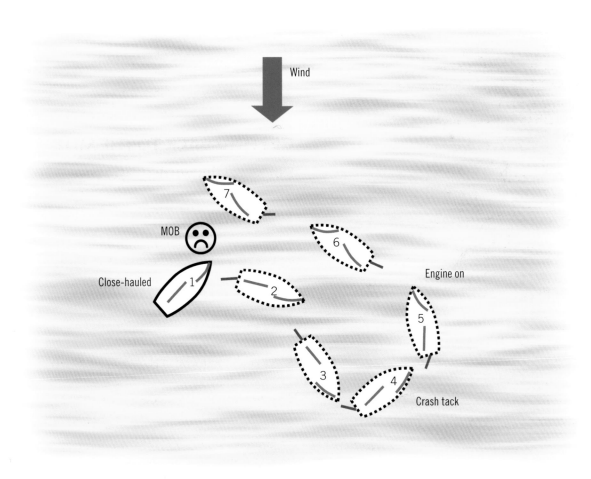

Windward MOB strategy 1

MAN OVERBOARD RETRIEVAL

- Buoy overboard with Lifesaver attached.

- The plan for getting back to the MOB.

- Approach the MOB by sailing to windward with a backed headsail.

- Heave to above the MOB.

- Get in position with the boathook.

- The Lifesaver makes it easy to grab the practice MOB.

Sailing to windward: strategy 2

If conditions are fairly light, rather than bear away on to a broad reach, I aim to spin the boat round and pick up the MOB:

1. Count to five and centre the main during this time.
2. Crash tack.
3. Keeping going round.
4. Run down with the headsail aback.
5. Start the engine.
6. Round up above the MOB into the heave-to position.

I need a little room for this, which is why I have a beat's pause while I count to five after the MOB has gone in, before crash tacking. This gives me the opportunity to make sure the main is centred, although I don't intend to gybe during this procedure. I will then crash tack and keep going through the tack with the headsail aback until I am more or less running dead downwind. I will start the engine now in case I need any help either to turn the boat up into the heave-to position or to remain hove-to and stopped in the water by the MOB.

Having an engine available means I can also simply motor back to the MOB, assuming I have white sails set. First I will make sure I have centred the main and furled the headsail. Now I can drive the boat where I like without worrying about the sails, the rig and gybing.

If the MOB went in when you were on a broad or beam reach then you'd round up, crash tack and sail back to him with the headsail aback and settle into the heave-to position to windward of him.

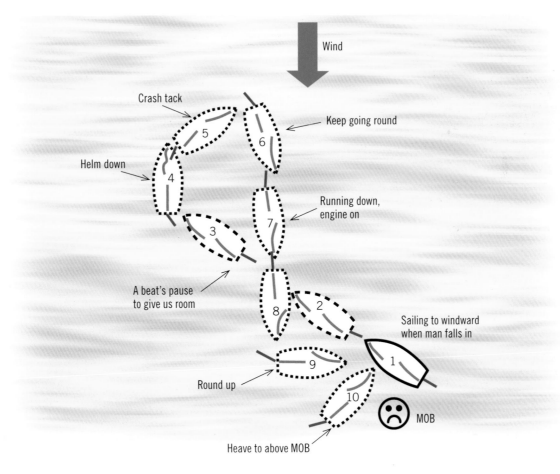

Windward MOB strategy 2

Sailing downwind under spinnaker

What if the MOB goes in when you have a spinnaker or cruising chute set? The first thing to do is to get the spinnaker or cruising chute down. You can do this one of two ways:

Method 1

1. Start the engine.
2. Leave the main out to blanket the spinnaker when you drop it.
3. Ease the guy so the spinnaker pole goes forward to the forestay.
4. Release the sheet to help de-power the sail.
5. Drop and gather the sail on deck, or snuff it if it has a snuffer.
6. Unclip the sheet and guy from the spinnaker pole and stow the pole on deck.
7. Get the spinnaker below if possible.
8. Centre the main and either motor or sail back under main to the MOB.

Method 2

1. Start the engine.
2. Centre the main.
3. Ease the guy so the spinnaker pole goes forward to the forestay.
4. Round up under engine.
5. The spinnaker will now be flattened against the mast and can be dropped.
6. Unclip the sheet and guy from the spinnaker pole and stow the pole on deck.
7. Get the spinnaker below if possible.
8. Either motor or sail back under main to the MOB.

Sailing downwind under cruising chute

Method 1

1. Start the engine.
2. Leave the main out to blanket the cruising chute.
3. Ease the sheet.
4. Snuff the sail.
5. Centre the main.
6. Leaving the cruising chute snuffed, motor or sail back under main to the MOB.

Method 2

1. Start the engine.
2. Centre the main.
3. Round up.
4. The cruising chute will be flattened against the mast and can be dropped or snuffed.
5. Motor or sail back to the MOB.

You'll probably have more success with dropping the spinnaker or cruising chute if you do this downwind with the sail blanketed by the main. I find I cannot get the boat head-to-wind when I have a large downwind sail set without the help of the engine. And even then the bow has a tendency to blow off. So doing any of this on your own in a hurry is not easy.

⌘ Cruising chute against mast ready to be dropped or snuffed.

For short-handed sailors, I'd recommend that any downwind sail should have either a snuffer or a furling system.

If you can't get your downwind sail down you may need to be prepared to let it go altogether. You can lose a spinnaker by letting off the guys and sheets and then releasing the halyard while running downwind. That's why you don't have stopper knots. Let it go overboard. You can collect it later after you have rescued your MOB.

With a cruising chute you have the added difficulty of the tack line running through a couple of blocks and this might snag. I would let the tack line go first, making sure that there was no stopper knot in the line. Then with the tack free, lose the halyard and sheets and it should fly away from the boat.

It is important to ensure that you have all lines, guys, sheets and so forth on board and nothing trailing in the water before you put the engine into gear. There's a lot of lengthy cordage associated with downwind sails.

These techniques for returning to the MOB need to be practised in all conditions for you to become comfortable with them and for them to begin to become second nature. Or, indeed, you may have another technique that you prefer. Whatever your strategy, practise, practise, practise. In light airs everything is fairly straightforward, but the minute the wind pipes up things take on quite a different complexion. You only have to present the wind with a scrap of sail or a beam-on topside for the boat to be off like a rocket and for you to be sailing away from the MOB.

⌘ Getting ready to lose the cruising chute. I hasten to add that I have not actually tried losing the spinnaker or cruising chute altogether, although I will one day.
Photo: © Rick Buettner

⌘ A snuffer is ideal for short-handers.
Photo: © Rick Buettner

GETTING AN ABLE MOB BACK ON BOARD

You have arrived with the MOB and are now hove-to. The MOB is keen to get back on board and as long as there is not so much movement that it would be dangerous, the MOB may be able to board by the stern over a sugar scoop or up a bathing ladder; otherwise he will have to be brought back on board amidships. Try to get a line to the MOB first, to keep him with the boat. The throwing line is probably easiest to get to him. Remember when throwing any line to throw it high so that it misses the guard rail. An under-arm throw is likely to be interrupted by the top guard rail!

Holding the boat alongside the MOB

The MOB may be attached to the boat with a line, but you don't want to go screaming around at a couple of knots dragging him through the water. The boat needs to be stopped. So make sure the balance between main and headsail is correct (furl or drop the headsail if necessary), the helm is down between 20° and 25° and perhaps ease the main a little, to ensure that you are hove to and doing less than 1 knot through the water. Again, you will have practised this and will have a good idea of the trim required to achieve this.

Mayday

The able MOB has fair screamed up the bathing ladder, just as relieved as you are that he is back on board and that the drama is over. It is not, though, because in UK and northern European waters an MOB calls for an immediate Mayday. You have about 15 minutes in our

cold waters before the mind becomes confused, the fingers stop working and hypothermia begins to set in. Added to which a person in the water experiences hydrostatic squeeze where the pressure of the water keeps some of the warm blood in around the vital organs while the blood on the outside cools.

Once out of the water the pressure releases and this warm blood can rush away from the organs and set off hypothermia or rush away from the heart, causing a massive lowering of the blood pressure and a heart attack. There is also the possibility of secondary drowning where the body sensing that the lungs have had some salt water in them will flush this out with water from within, which can drown a person. So medical advice is required quickly. Calling a Mayday you can relay the condition of your MOB to people who know. They may decide to have him airlifted to hospital.

GETTING AN UNCONSCIOUS MOB BACK ON BOARD

We must always prepare for the worst. What if the MOB couldn't help himself? He's fallen in why? Lost his balance? Did he hit his head on anything as he went over? Heart attack? Perhaps the shock of the cold water has stunned him or he might be suffering from hypothermia. Now the MOB is comatose and you have to get him back on board on your own. This is everyone's worst nightmare.

Let's assume the MOB is wearing a life jacket and is floating the right way up. If he is not wearing a life jacket... well, we'll come to that in a minute.

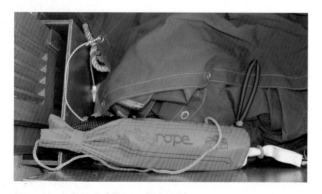

Try to get a throwing line to the MOB

Why do we shiver?

We shiver because the skin has become too cool and has sent a signal to the brain that we need to warm up. The brain then starts the muscles expanding and contracting and this twitching effect produces heat.

The conditions, strength of the wind and sea state make an enormous difference to this operation. The less of everything, the better. The more, the harder it will be and the more careful you have to be of not injuring the MOB with the boat.

Once you are with the MOB you need to attach him to the boat while you set up whatever retrieval system you are going to use. But how are you going to attach the comatose MOB to the boat? Even if you can get a boathook tucked into the webbing of the life jacket, what are you going to do next? If the life jacket has a D-ring it will be under the inflated bladder, out of sight and impossible to hook with the boathook. Can you lasso a line around the MOB? He is comatose, remember, and cannot help. How can you get a line down to the MOB? Your arms will not stretch (see Table below). You cannot reach him.

MOB Lifesavers from Duncan Wells

This is why I have invented the Lifesaver. I have been mulling over this conundrum of how to get a line on to an MOB for years. I have discussed it with many instructors who specialise in MOB solutions and systems for retrieval and no one has been able to work out how we get a line on to the MOB.

The D-ring is under the inflated bladder

With the Lifesaver you don't go down to the MOB, he comes up to you. Instead of trying to get a line down on to the MOB, you get a line from him up to you. A Lifesaver is a spliced loop of dayglo Dyneema, 1.5m in length, with a triangle formed in one end. The Lifesaver is attached to the lifting becket in the life jacket and tucked inside the cover.

When the life jacket deploys the Lifesaver floats out onto the water. Now you just lift the Lifesaver out with the boathook and attach it to a cleat to hold the MOB alongside while you set up your retrieval system. For life jackets that have two lifting straps, identified by having 2 'D' rings, you attach a Lifesaver to each strap and bring them out on the two Lifesavers.

The height of gunwhale from the water when the boat is level	
Halberg Rassy 352	110cm
Dufour 375	120cm
Bavaria 42	127cm
Bavaria 36	110cm
Hanse 414	145cm
Oyster 65	145cm
Rustler 36	80cm

▶ *Lifesaver, a means to get a line from the MOB to the boat (www.moblifesavers.com)*

▶▶ *The Lifesaver line is attached to the becket of the lifting strop inside the life jacket*

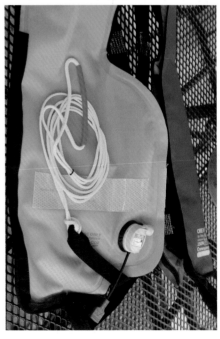

MOB LIFESAVER IN ACTION

■ Man overboard!

■ The life jacket has inflated and the Lifesaver line is clearly visible. Note how the Lifesaver line floats away from the MOB, giving the rescuer plenty to aim at with the boathook.

■ The rescuer hooks the line with the boathook.

■ And gets it on board.

■ The line can then be made fast on a cleat and the MOB is securely attached to the boat.

■ And a retrieval system is rigged.

Once you've got the MOB attached, it's time to winch him on board. Consider losing the guard wires as you won't have to winch the MOB so high and you can roll him in over the gunwhale. A Lifesaver is capable of lifting a Mini Cooper car and 4 adults, so it'll manage a MOB. In fact the lifting strop in the life jacket is only rated at 326.5kg. I say 'only', but that is 51 stone and so the life jacket would give up long before the Lifesaver.

Retrieval systems

For years I have had a four-part tackle, a handy billy, assembled and ready to go. It took five minutes to rig. I now have a couple of much simpler systems. The first makes use of the extraordinary properties of Dyneema. This system takes less than two minutes to rig and uses one block, one short loop of Dyneema, one turning block, one line with a carabiner attached and one longer loop of Dyneema to be used as a step (see box overleaf for step-by-step instructions).

I can actually set this up in 1 minute and 15 seconds. What takes the longest time is uncoiling the line, even when it is coiled the climber's way. I suggest you have a specific line for this at just the length you need – from gunwhale to the block, down to the turning block, through the sheet leads on the genoa track, up to the cockpit winch and enough for a few turns on, plus a metre spare in case. With the carabiner tied into this permanently, this is ready to go and will deploy quickly. The load for this set-up is taken directly in line with the cap shroud.

▲ Winching the MOB on board. If we have lines led to the cockpit as opposed to lines led to the mast our retrieval rig is set up for us, as we will use the spinnaker halyard or a spare jib halyard which we can load onto a cockpit winch. Even though we don't need to set up a rig, we do need to establish which system we will use and practise it.

▶ Block raised on the spinnaker halyard with the line led to a turning block at the base of the shroud to prevent the halyard from pulling on the spreader

MAKING A SIMPLE RETRIEVAL SYSTEM

■ The ingredients. The short loop of Dyneema is already attached to the block.

■ The block is attached to the cap shroud with a Klemheist knot (see Chapter 2). A length of clear PVC tubing over the stainless steel of the shroud will allow the knot to lock.

■ Use a snatch block with snap shackle for the turning block, attach this to the bottle screw at the base of the shroud and reeve the line through this and the blocks on the genoa sheet lead back to the cockpit winch.

■ Notice how the load will be taken down the length of the cap shroud.

■ You now need to raise the block on the shroud with the Dyneema. You can push a Klemheist knot up but when tension is applied to the knot, it locks.

■ If you're short you can make a step up using Dyneema. Take the other loop, tie a Klemheist knot around the cap shroud, allow enough spare to get your foot into it and then you can step up. You could always make another step above this if need be.

■ By using the step even a short crew can get the block on the Klemheist knot well up the shroud – high enough to be able to lift out the MOB.

The second system uses the spinnaker halyard and requires one block, one line with a carabiner tied into the end, one turning block and of course the spinnaker halyard.
To set this up:

- Attach the snatch block to the bottle screw at the base of the cap shroud; you are going to use this as a turning block, as before.
- Reeve the line through the block, the turning block and through the blocks on the genoa sheet lead track and up to the cockpit.
- Clip the carabiner to the upper guard wire.
- Take the spinnaker halyard and clip the snap shackle to the block.
- Checking that you have led the rig correctly through the stays and that the spinnaker halyard is forward of the spreader, raise the spinnaker halyard to your pre-determined mark.

Using the spinnaker halyard, why not reeve the line through the block in advance?

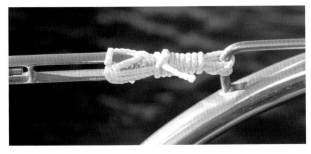

The guard wire is attached with a lashing which can be cut to allow easier retrieval of the MOB

Always use a turning block at the base of the cap shroud rather than lead the line to the first block on the genoa sheet lead, to ensure that the lifting load comes straight down and does not put any pressure on the spreader.

Now take the Lifesaver off the cleat and attach the carabiner. Finally, before any winching in, cut the lashing for the lower guard wire. Keep the upper guard wire in place especially if the boat is moving about a bit as it will afford you some security – if you can't get the MOB over the gunwhale with it in place that is the time to lose it. Load the winch with four turns and start to winch your MOB out.

My kit is kept together and ready to deploy in an instant. And that is it. The 5mm Dyneema loop, even knotted, is capable of lifting several tons so it is plenty strong enough and the Klemheist knot holds it rock steady on the shroud. Quick, easy, simple. I keep the line with the carabiner already tied into the snatch block with the loop of Dyneema, ready to hand.

If you're using the spinnaker halyard to raise the block, then you need to make sure that the spinnaker halyard block at the top of the mast and the halyard itself are in good condition and up to the job. A rig check is always a good idea.

Klemheist and Prusik knots seem to grip to anything when a load is applied instantly. They can slip when the load is applied gradually on stainless steel, because of the twist of the wire. If we sheath the stainless steel in a PVC tube this stops the slippage.

Handy billy assembly   **TOP TIP**

When assembling four-part tackles (also known as a handy billy), use at least one fiddle block, preferably two, as you don't want the falls to twist, which they can do when you use double blocks.

Scan this QR code to watch a video on retrieval rig options.

Scan this QR code to watch a video on Lifesavers.

And that is how to retrieve the MOB on board. I tested this out. I am not standing on anything or leaning on anything. I am just hanging there. It was not in the least bit uncomfortable

Raising the MOB to slow hypothermia

You don't want the MOB in the water for longer than necessary. Search and rescue paramedics advise that, if at all possible, it would be a good idea to raise the MOB out of the water while setting up the retrieval system. Getting the torso out of the water could help to slow down the onset of hypothermia, as long as the wind isn't colder than the water, in which case leaving him in the water might be best.

Attach a line to the MOB's Lifesaver and load this on to the winch on the opposite side of the cockpit to the MOB (the 3mm Dyneema won't load on to a winch)

and winch him up. It may be possible to winch him back on board this way without the need for setting up the retrieval tackle.

This is something to test out on a fine day in the summer. First lose the guard wires. Then get a crew member, dressed in a life jacket, to lie on the dock. Open out the life jacket and attach a Lifesaver to the lifting becket. Bring this over the gunwhale, attach a line to the Lifesaver and load this line on to a winch on the far side of the cockpit. Now winch away and watch as the MOB is raised up and over the gunwhale. I tried this. It was not too uncomfortable.

Short-handed considerations

With a full crew, we would have someone pointing at the MOB the whole time, someone would have hit the MOB button on the GPS/plotter, someone would have thrown the throwing line, someone would have littered the water with detritus, someone would have turned on the engine and someone would be getting out the four-part tackle for retrieval. But you don't have someone to help. You're on your own so you need to make sure you don't lose sight of the MOB despite the fact that you are doing many other things at the same time.

If the MOB is wearing a life jacket with a Lifesaver in and you are going to turn the boat straight round and go back to him without touching the sheets, there isn't a great deal to do except keep your eyes glued to him. You'll need the boathook to hand as you come alongside, but that should always be kept in the same place, for example on the coach roof. So with the boat alongside, you step out of the cockpit, grab the boathook and get hold of the Lifesaver floating on the water.

Talk to the MOB

Don't forget to talk to the MOB all the time. Tell him you are coming back for him. Tell him what you are about to do. He might regain consciousness and be able to help and if not, even if he is comatose, he may still be able to hear. Encourage him. Telling him what you are doing will help you to remember the steps you need to take. After all, you will be in a state of panic and it will help to focus the mind.

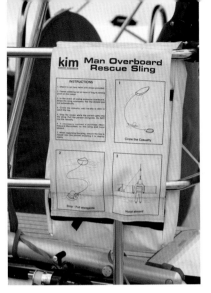

⌘ Rescue sling.

⌘ Pick-up sail.

⌘ The sail does not sink and so it is difficult to get an incapacitated casualty into it.

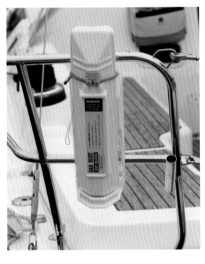

⌘ Jonbuoy.

⌘ Lifting line.

Man overboard devices

There are a number of products and techniques out there which are designed to help in recovering the MOB to the boat and the retrieval on board:

- Rescue slings, Oscar slings, Seattle slings
- Jonbuoy, Danbuoy
- MOB mats, pick-up sails
- Safety ladders
- Lifting line

Not one of them works for a comatose MOB and several of them don't work very well for able MOBs, which is why the Lifesaver came about. Even with an able MOB it may well be that boarding by the stern via a bathing ladder or sugar scoop is too dangerous given the sea state and so they can be hoisted on board amidships, using the Lifesaver.

Being attached to the the becket of the lifting strop on a life jacket you will be lifted more or less vertically out of the water. Ideally, an MOB should be lifted horizontally to prevent the blood rushing from the heart to the legs. The only thing to say is that with the Lifesaver we hope to be in a position to lift the MOB out of the water much sooner than if we were trying to get him out with a MOB mat or similar and so one might hope that his body temperature had not fallen so low that the hydrostatic squeeze from the water was the only thing keeping warm blood around his heart.

If you need to lift the MOB out horizontally you can employ a strop behind the knees. You can use the heavyweight lasso (see Chapter 6) which will sink under him, bring this behind his knees, add this into the carabiner that's lifting him and bring him out in the sitting position, or possibly horizontal.

If the mob is not wearing a life jacket

This is very difficult indeed.

Using a dinghy

If you have a dinghy to hand all well and good. You could launch this, making sure it is attached to the boat, and then you would try to roll the MOB into the dinghy. Rescue services use RIBs to retrieve MOBs and they deflate a sponson to make it easier to roll them in. But they have crew who can act as a counterweight as the MOB is brought aboard. You do not. It is very likely that you'd capsize the dinghy trying to roll the MOB in.

Using a liferaft

This is possible, although getting into the liferaft will be difficult. Attach the liferaft to the boat by another means than the existing painter as there is a set-breaking load that the rubber patch holding the painter to the liferaft will detach at and you wouldn't want to find that neither the MOB in the water nor yourself in the liferaft were attached to the boat.

Getting into the water with the MOB

This is extremely dangerous. Of course, we will do anything to save our partner and if they were unconscious and it was summer time and the boat was not moving about a great deal it may be possible to get into the water with a line attached in order to attach a harness or couple of ropes to the MOB. This would be an occasion when a bowline in a doubled line would be useful. The beauty of this is that you end up with a loop to go under the armpits, a loop to go behind the knees and a nice little loop to attach the carabiner.

Getting into the water with the MOB is very likely to end up badly. But if one of my family was unconscious in the water and drowning, I'd be in there like a shot, or rather as soon after I had tied myself to the boat.

The long and short of it all is to have a strategy, to practise getting back to an MOB (invest in a little buoy and use some old rope for the MOB) and to practise the retrieval. And then you've done the best you can to prepare for something that will hopefully never happen.

◀ *Using a heavyweight lasso to lift the MOB horizontally*

▼ *Bowline in a doubled line*

Rough, cold sea of the inner walkway at Corbiere, Jersey

TEMPERATURE AND THE BODY

Normal body temperature	98.6°F (37°C)
Hypothermia sets in	95°F (35°C)
Mental capacity lost	93°F (33.9°C)
Unconscious	86°F (30°C)
Dead	80°F (26.7°C)
Cold water definition	<25°C
UK sea water temperature minimum (February)	5°C
UK sea water temperature maximum (August)	19°C

Temperature and the body

The table to the left shows what happens to the human body at various temperatures. Interestingly, the temperature in the Solent when we were testing the Lifesavers in the summer of 2014, with Alan & Liam from Hamble Lifeboat, was 21°C. Much warmer than it should have been, in fact not in the least bit unpleasant. And yes, I went in twice for the cause. After all I couldn't ask anyone else to do what I was not prepared to do myself.

GLOSSARY

Aback	Sheeted off on the windward side, as opposed to the leeward side
Crash tack	To tack without touching the headsail sheet so that the headsail is aback when you are on the new tack
Helm down	The tiller has been turned to leeward, the rudder will turn the boat to windward. A wheel helm turns to windward to achieve this
Helm up	The tiller has been turned to windward, the rudder will turn the boat to leeward. A wheel helm turns to leeward to achieve this
White sails	Any sail other an asymmetric, gennaker, cruising chute or a spinnaker (a racing expression, in a white sails race no one is allowed to use a spinnaker)

EPILOGUE

I hope that you will have found some techniques here that you can use to make your boating stress-free and therefore more enjoyable. Nobody wants to arrive at the marina dreading the departure and if you practise one or two of the techniques and become confident you can reduce the worry of it considerably. If you are confident that you can get off the dock on your own and confident that you can get back on to it on your own, then you are in business and there will be a good deal less shouting in the average marina on a Sunday evening.

Apart from the techniques, preparation is key to the success of any boating operation. Working to systems is important, too. If you know the procedure before you start and everything is to hand where you know it will be, life will run smoothly on board.

It really is worth taking time to practise. I know we have very little time available for sailing, but practising coming on and off the berth, sailing in a circle, heaving to, reefing and picking up mooring buoys will pay dividends. I am pretty good at handling my car. Why? Because I do it every day. I sail my boat once a week if I am very lucky, usually less often. So I need to practise.

It is also very important to investigate the options for man overboard retrieval and find one that you like and then practise rigging it while timing yourself. Should an emergency arise, you'll be ready for it.

There is fabulous fun to be had out there on the water. And now we have taken some of the stress out of it, we can enjoy it even more.

Back in safe, time for a gin

INDEX